What Do You Know?

Congratulations — 2005!

Jeanette Berry Spires

*Inspiration and Advice
for Young People from
53 Exceptional Americans*

What Do You Know?

Wisdom for the Road Ahead

Edited by
JEANETTE SPIRES

Foreword by
STUART SCOTT

RIVERWOOD BOOKS
ASHLAND, OREGON

RiverWood Books, PO Box 3400, Ashland, Oregon 97520
www.riverwoodbooks.com

Printed in Indonesia

First edition: 2003

Cover design by David Ruppe, Impact Publications

Library of Congress Cataloging-in-Publication Data
Spires, Jeanette.
    What Do You Know? : wisdom for the road ahead / by Jeanette Spires & 53 exceptional Americans ; foreword by Stuart Scott.
        p. cm.
    ISBN 1-883991-75-7
    1. High school graduates--Conduct of life. 2. Young adults--Conduct of life.

    BJ1661.W43 2003
    646.7'00835--dc21
                                                        2002037104

06 05 04 03   9 8 7 6 5 4 3 2 1

Contents

Relationships

Exploring the World

Mind and Body

Trials

Foreword

"AAARRRGGGGHHHH! HELP!
I'm 18. What the heck do I do now?"

That, in so many words, was my first thought the summer I turned 18. The summer before my freshman year at UNC-Chapel Hill. Of course, I didn't TELL anyone that thought. Come on, I was a football player. I was a MAN (or so I thought.) I couldn't EXPRESS any apprehension. Oh, but I felt it. Just like every other 18-year old. Officially, you're an adult…unofficially, you're at the infancy of a world of responsibility, happiness, contentment, heartache, intrigue…and somewhere along the way…the education, required, to admit that UNCERTAINTY you're feeling right now…is OK.

This book is based on a story about a young man celebrating his 18th birthday when his uncle came up and said what ALL uncles and fathers and grandfathers say:

"If I could be 18 again and know what I know now…"—to which the young man responded, "Well, I'm 18! What do you know?" This book will try to answer that question. Here's what I remember about being 18…I pretty much IGNORED the advice of my elders, at least to their faces. That whole macho thing, again. But every once in a while, what was said to me made a TINY bit of sense. I'll come clean…I was a little curious.

So are you. Does that mean you'll sit down right now and read this from front to back? Probably not, and even if you did, the lessons in these words are probably better taught by experiencing them than reading ABOUT them. It's why GOD makes us feel like we're invincible at 18. I take far fewer chances in life NOW, understanding my own mortality, than I did at 18. But had I not taken those chances THEN, I would never have achieved the personal and business successes I've had. Life is tough and rewarding at the same time, bitter...and sweet. Within these pages, the gracious contributors share their lessons, mistakes, and accomplishments. Learn from them. Learn ABOUT them. An open mind: an open heart. Who knows, in 18 years, when YOU'RE 36, you might be imparting the same lessons. Peace.

Stuart Scott
ESPN "SportsCenter" Anchor

Appearances

A primitive kind of sorting out through
appearances goes on
every day of your
life.
Deciding how to balance
externals and internals
is part of the work
of growing up.

Master That Grip

by Marjabelle Young Stewart

Widely considered America's leading authority on manners, Marjabelle is the author of numerous books on etiquette, the latest being *Common Sense Etiquette*. She is a veteran of the interview, having been featured on "The Tonight Show," "The Today Show," "Good Morning America," "The Oprah Winfrey Show," and many others. As a regular on "The Howie Mandel Show," she countered Howie's good-natured befuddlement over correct manners with charm and zest. Dave Barry wrote a column about lunch with Marjabelle: "She turned out to be a perfectly sane, relentlessly cheerful lady who believes in saying nice things about everybody, including New Yorkers, and who believes that the most important thing in the world is good manners."

Marjabelle began her career by teaching classes in etiquette to children in Washington, D.C., and her etiquette book for children is in its 35th year in print. Called The Queen of Courtesy, her annual poll of America's Most Polite Cities is gratefully received by the mayors of the cities that make the list..

One of Marjabelle's greatest pleasures is working with college students in seminars for job-seekers, especially those fraternity types who want to put Animal House behind them.

CARY GRANT ONCE told me that when he began acting in films, he had no idea how a gentleman behaved. His early film directors had to teach him the fine points of elegant behavior. He admitted, "I acted like a gentleman for so long I just became one."

You become as you act. In over 30 years of monitoring America's manners, I have learned that you can overcome all kinds of difficulties in your background by learning and then practicing the rules of social behavior. Good manners reflect consideration that originates in thinking about making others comfortable. Just as you learn the rules for math, grammar and games, you can open doors for yourself by knowing social rules. Without knowing the rules, you are walking in a social mine field. If you have good manners, you make others comfortable, which reflects a basic respect for all people.

A CEO of a large corporation that requires its executives to travel abroad pointed out, "You have to have the look of a good upbringing." If you play golf or tennis, you know the importance of the right grip. If a prospective employer takes you to lunch, you don't want to have a power failure at the table. There is an art to correct dining—sets of tools that can be mastered—and the rules are readily available in your library. Animals eat; people dine.

After World War II, the world opened up to commerce and development. As a nation, we didn't take time to consider the rules and justly earned an "Ugly American" title. When I instruct a new class of MBA recipients about etiquette, they are immediately empowered in their ability to show their respect for others in a positive way. Good manners will take you farther than a Rolex watch will. This is a society which allows people to blossom. You have an inalienable right to be well-bred.

Your Image Counts

by Anna Wildermuth

Experiences in early life that caused us consternation may become the driving force behind the deep satisfaction of true fit in a career. Anna's essay provides personal insight into her own path. Anna is a certified image consultant, a graduate of the London Image Institute in Atlanta. She is an expert on the psychology and color of clothing combined with the power of communication.

As an accomplished photographer and floral designer, her natural flair for composition causes her to look at you as a living work of art. Anna works on the visual image of her client; she educates anyone from the president of a large corporation to a teen working toward high school equivalency and an entry level job. Her company, Personal Images, Inc. (personalimagesinc.com), can provide training designed to bring out the best in people.

SPEAKING FROM MY own experience, beginning the ongoing process of developing an authentic visual image is critical at age 18. This is the beginning of your adulthood, whether you are going to college or interviewing for a job. You want to make a good impression based on your appearance, your body language, the tone of your voice and what you say.

As I look back on my late teens, I think my image was that of a good student who was active in school, but fit in better academically than socially. Although my neighborhood was considered to be very affluent, my family had little money. My parents were first generation Chinese and we lived behind a laundry. My friends all lived in nice houses or expensive condos. Socially, I was exposed to highly intelligent people, wonderful homes and fine dining. Did I have an opportunity to develop a visual image that was really me? No, not during those times. I worked too hard to make up for not belonging. I wanted the look of affluence and tried to show my intelligence by behaving and dressing like my smart friends.

Today, I know better. Your visual image needs to be tied to who you are. Here are some rules you can adapt to work for you:

1. Love your heritage—it helps you understand your inherent physical qualities.

2. Develop good grooming habits, a key component of coming from good "stock."

3. Accept the shape and height of your body. Look for people who have the same coloring and body shape and whose appearance you admire.

4. Stand up straight, enunciate when you speak, and have good eye contact. Engaging others with your energy makes them feel respected.

5. Better clothing is more important than lots of clothing. Fit is important: not too tight or too big. Make sure the item of clothing you are purchasing works with at least three items already in your closet.

6. Don't be swayed by the desire to "be in" all the time. "In" becomes "Out" very quickly, and that money could have been invested in a higher quality item.

7. Learn to develop style. When you feel good about your appearance, you will feel good about yourself.

8. Remember you are not the exception to the rule. Understand what is appropriate for where you are, whether in a job interview or in school.

Your image is your impact. Others may make decisions about you in ten seconds. Let your outer person reflect the wonderful inner person you are.

First Impressions

by Paula Zahn

Do you ever meet someone, form an instant opinion, and tuck that person into a compartment labeled "not worth further investigation"? Paula's observations about first impressions will cause you to stop and think before you prejudge a person.

Interviews are a formality of life that can strike fear into the heart of the job hunter. Watching a master interviewer like Paula Zahn can show you how to think on your feet. Before she interviews a subject, she does extensive research, just as you must do before you step into the shoes of the job candidate. No one seems to rattle Paula's composure because she is prepared. Even when she probes into sensitive information, she remains respectful and sticks to facts.

Paula attended Stephens College and landed her first media job in a Dallas station. She has covered the Olympics, hosted major network morning shows and won a number of Emmy Awards for her investigative reporting and coverage of ongoing news stories.

Amidst all of this activity, her three children take priority. An award which makes her most proud could be her recognition of one of the 1992 Mothers of the Year by the National Mother's Day Committee.

As a journalist, I have interviewed thousands of people. My job is to go beyond obvious rote questions, and ask questions that will elicit new information and help viewers gain fresh insights into my interviewee. And while every interview requires a unique approach, I have learned some techniques that are effective most of the time. I try not to prejudge the person I will interview. First impressions are often wrong. Most folks who are being interviewed for the first time have their guard up, and for good reason. It is very difficult to trust someone you've never met. I also think it's critical that you do your homework. Interviewees are immediately turned off by people who don't prepare. The best way to pierce someone's reserve is to prove to them that you know your stuff. Once someone respects you they will be far more willing to open up with you.

Humor is also a very important part of communicating with someone. Let's face it, we all have our hang-ups and vulnerabilities. And, it can be very disarming to someone if you are honest about your fears or insecurities. People like to be "let in." You just have to make sure that in opening up yourself you aren't self-absorbed. You can quickly turn people off if you don't show any interest in their lives.

So as you go out into the world and try to make your mark, just remember to hold back your judgment of others until you've had a chance to come to your own conclusions by talking and sharing with them. More often than not, when I've had a negative impression of someone going into an interview (based on what I had read about them), I walk away with a different view. The only impression that counts is one that follows honest interaction.

My final piece of advice to you—keep in mind as you try to dazzle a potential employer or suitor with your brilliance and wit, that a phony can be spotted from miles away. Don't try to be someone you are not. Be comfortable in your own skin. When you are relaxed and confident with who you are, people will respond in kind. You only get as good as you give.

Respect for Other

There's a tendency to seek out
people most like yourself.
What do you lose
by keeping your protective covering
so tight?

Eye Contact

by Keith Barkley

Keith Barkley grew up on a family farm near Grinnell, Iowa. He studied industrial economics at Iowa State University, spent five years in the U.S. Air Force, and somewhere along the line, became an ordained Presbyterian minister. Keith's most dramatic adventures occurred late in his career when he took the unusual step of becoming an overseas missionary.

Keith went to Africa to help a rural Kenyan village obtain safe drinking water, raising money from across the United States to help accomplish this goal. He educated himself in water engineering from texts he brought along, and lived for several years in a small shack in a village that had no electricity or other modern amenities. Keith recalls the joy of living in the African village where community and social relationships are paramount. Today, he maintains those relationships with his friends in Kenya from his current home in Colorado.

His young dark eyes and my old pale blue eyes met, locked for an eternal, paralyzing second, then darted apart, mutually embarrassed. For lack of knowing the nine year-old peasant boy's name, I'll call him Samuel.

Into Samuel's poor, densely populated East African rural village, about six of us from the developed world had come to hold 12 village-wide meetings over a five day period. We were joined by with five young African volunteers with meager experience in rural "bootstrap" development. Community problems and deficiencies were listed on a blackboard:

"There isn't enough food."

"We walk long distances for unhealthy water."

"No money, no jobs, no transportation, no real road."

"Drought is a problem."

"Our agriculture is primitive, done mostly by manual labor—and even new jembes (hoes) and pangas (machetes) we cannot afford."

"Tse-Tse flies and ticks kill our cattle."

"Our schools are very weak, without books, and we have few trained teachers."

"For lack of a health clinic, many people die at the witch doctor's compound."

"Malaria and dysentery kill too many children."

"Our mud and grass houses are unhealthy."

"Politicians and other 'big men' abuse us and rob us."

During the next five days we debated and established priorities, apportioned scarce resources, discussed and adopted village strategies, chose prime movers, and finalized tactics and schedules. We took at least a first step on the bumpy road of self-help by disempowered people.

The culminating event of development planning was a village-wide celebration and feast, beginning with rousing, congratulatory, hope-inspiring "official" oratory that was followed by equally long and even more flowery responses by the best village orators. Not being one of the speakers, I had made my introverted North American white face as backrowish and inconspicuous as possible. During the interlude following the oratory, I judged the verbal buzz (in the local tribal language, of which I caught only a few words) to be one-third optimistic, and two-thirds pessimistic. The elders were near totally unmoved: to the well of unfulfilled promises they had been led too many times. Yet nearly everyone clung to some shred of dubious hope that for the children at least, life could possibly get a little better.

The "feast" consisted of two-to-three pieces of boiled goat (including certain of the innards) and boiled corn meal. Children and nursing mothers were served first; few had spoons, fingers sufficed. Against the wall on the far side of the room, seated on the top board of a bleacher, sat Samuel in his tattered, buttonless, oversized hand-me-down shirt. He was finishing his portion of the feast and obviously having enjoyed it had wiped clean the inside of the serving bowl with his forefinger. Just as he raised his finger to his mouth for the last time, he sensed that he was being observed intensely—even spied upon. Looking up to locate his intruder, he found me. Our eyes met and locked for only a microsecond, but for me that was an emotional eternity. Samuel's face was filled with horror. It was as if by failing to conceal his hunger in a white man's presence, he had embodied — even contributed to — all of Africa's current failings.

I wanted to reach across that room, grab Samuel by the shoulders and say, "Samuel, it is I rather than you who is to be ashamed — I of first world affluence and indifference who has done virtually nothing, and taken so long to get here." But there was nothing that I could do. Had I started towards him, Samuel would have fled out into the night. There was just nothing I could do except to remember that brief instant of eye contact.

All of that was 20 years ago. I was a man, Samuel a boy, and it was he who taught me and changed my life. Often have I thought of Samuel. Is he alive today? Or did malaria, dysentery, untreated injury, violence or war claim his life in his teenage years? There is no way Samuel can know that he affected me such that six years later, I returned to an even drier, poorer region of Kenya, 300 miles from Samuel's village, and there labored for nearly five years to help 12,000 rural villagers obtain safe drinking water.

Today we are advised to avoid eye contact with strangers when walking U.S. city streets; "You may trigger some misinterpreting 'contactee', or some enraged youth." Maybe so. Probably this is sound, cautious advice that I may someday convey to my young grandchildren. But for me, that one brief eye contact with a small African boy years ago I will remember ever and gratefully.

We Are All Related

by Albert White Hat, Sr.

A Lakota Chief, Albert White Hat, Sr., carries the traditions of his people to the next generation as an instructor in Lakota Studies at Sinte Gleska University in Rosebud, South Dakota. Sinte Gleska is one of 29 tribal colleges in the United States that educates young Native Americans and helps research and retain their history.

The Rosebud Sioux Reservation draws many visitors every year to the famed Sundance ceremonies—sacred rituals for the Lakota. Members of the tribe who live far away make an effort to return for the renewal ceremonies that take place each summer. Serious students of religion from all over the globe respectfully leave their cameras home and come to absorb the religious dances, rituals and the retelling of ancient stories.

Albert was crowned a chief of the Lakota Tribe at the annual Sundance in 1998. He can often be found moving among the visitors, earnestly explaining the ancient beliefs and accomplishments of his people, representing an unbroken tie to his ancestors.

REGARDLESS OF WHO people are or where they come from, everybody needs to be acknowledged. Our educational institutions from kindergarten to college focus just on the achievers. Many people are lost because no one has confirmed their worth and tried to help them. The system makes them feel stupid and unimportant. For example, many people feel sensitive about their appearance. They want to fit in and be part of things. This applies especially to people of color.

I grew up with the knowledge of my family. My mother taught me the history of my grandfather and great-grandfather. They were achievers and proud. I was firmly grounded in my culture and family history. It was customary in the area where I grew up to send children to boarding school when they were five years old and teach them until they were 18. I did not go to boarding school until I was 16. My peers nearly killed me because they were being taught to reject the Indian culture, and I was proud of my heritage. It is so obvious to Native Americans that we are not wanted by a society which is so steeped in western philosophy.

One summer, I hand picked five young boys who were delinquent. We put up a tepee; they cooked and cared for horses. I got the chance to say, "This is where you come from, your grandfathers did this, your great-grandfathers accomplished that." Even though they have continued to struggle, they still come to see me and shake my hand because I didn't baby them.

If you feel like an outcast in a society which is not really yours, you must research and learn about your roots. Learn the dances, songs and rituals. You may not realize that there was a time when the whole philosophy of my people was outlawed by this country. Finally, Congress passed a Freedom of Indian Religion Act. People in the past, trying to impose their ways of thought, even accused us of "devil worship." Through our rituals we have a sense of our relationship to creation. We're all related as humans to creation and to one another. It is not possible to be alone in this world, because the earth, trees and sky are all related to you. You can find peace by listening to the world around you.

Everything Knows You

by Theresa Arevgaq John

If you find yourself in Alaska, Theresa's one-woman show, Yup'ik Arnaq, will introduce you to her culture in a delightful way. In her current position on the faculty at Alaska Pacific University, she teaches a course called Native Ways of Knowing. She surprises her students every day with the intricacies of her upbringing and the intense spirituality of her native culture.

Theresa has performed native dance in locations as far-flung as Greenland, Greece, and the International Sacred Sites Festival in Machu Picchu. Her upbringing includes an important concept necessary to the survival of an ancient culture. The word upterrlainarluta means "always getting ready." Planning ahead for the long winter means constant preparation. She still loves to hunt and gather food, take steam baths and engage in dialogue with her elders.

Theresa stresses that we are all lifelong learners and that it is important to share our wisdom with others so that we all live in peace and harmony.

ALASKA IS OUR largest state, and although you may think we are all alike up here, there are five major ethnic groups who speak different dialects. I was born and raised on Nelson Island in a fishing village. I'm a Yup'ik and was raised in my culture in a pure way, not contaminated by the ideas of the outside world. Our culture is a spiritual one. Ellam Yua is our name for the Creator, who looks over everybody everywhere and has given us our way of living, our ways of healing, and our ways of celebrating. We believe that our souls and our beings never die. We are all ancestral spirits reincarnated. I am named for a great aunt, (my Yup'ik name is Arevgaq), the sister of my grandmother. When I visit my village, her children call me "Mom" in respect to her spirit within me.

Because we have an oral tradition, we instruct the children to remember what they have heard from their elders. In our culture, children are included in everything. Families are strong. My parents always invited elders to our home. They would tell us, "You are not going to understand this right now, but when you need to know, you will know." I still hunger for the lesson hour, and I still go to the Alaska Native Medical Center to find elders from whom I can both learn from and assist.

My students from down below who have come to Alaska Pacific are excited to learn of our teachings and the strength of our culture. A profound respect for the earth, the wind and the cosmos runs through our lives every moment. We don't waste anything. We believe that the caribou, the moose and all living things have spirits who observe and report on us — how we have treated them and whether we have respected what they have given us. I love my students, and I love passing on our culture to them.

What do I have to say to a young person just starting the path to becoming an elder? Respect everything Ellam Yua has given you, care for the earth and cherish the wisdom of your elders.

I Never Met a Stranger

by Mary Prentice

Mary Prentice is an educator of the gifted. Having tackled Rice University at the age of 15, she has the credentials to operate in a field where brainpower is important. She has studied in England, Spain, Scotland, and Greece. When she was a young woman, she lived in Brazil as part of a husband and wife missionary team. Mary started schools where there had never been formal education. She says her eyes were opened by living among people she [had] thought of as uneducated. She feels strongly that people we often think of as primitive are both smart and wise. They learn to survive in ways that we in our materialistic society never could.

Back in the U.S., she worked with the Missouri Association for Migrant Opportunity Services, a program which teaches migrant workers to read and write. When others might think of retirement, Mary entered Purdue University to earn her doctorate in the education of the gifted, and became the director of gifted education in Indiana. As an associate professor at the University of Arkansas-Little Rock, she wrote books on [applying multiple intelligence theory] in the classroom. [A]t the age of 70 she began a new job with Environmental and Spatial Technology to bring innovation to classroom teaching all over America. Mary wants people to discover who they are and why they are here, and then how to make the most of every opportunity.

WHEN I WAS A CHILD, I liked fried chicken, hot rolls, cream gravy and the preacher. I liked them in that order. Truth is, the reason I liked the preacher was that because of him we had the other. One Sunday as I walked through the kitchen door, I saw my mother showing the preacher a tablecloth my grandmother had made. It was a masterpiece of beauty with more than a hundred roses in various shades around the edges, and the leaves were a green I can still remember when I close my eyes.

I was horrified and hid, and watched from a distance. You see, some weeks before I had spilled some tea on it and it was now stained. As a child of seven, I just knew that the preacher would tell God and I would be in big trouble. I ran out the back door, got on my pony and rode to the hills. In those days we returned to the church in the late afternoon for a children's service. We went down to the front of the church that Sunday, and much to my absolute horror the preacher reached behind the pulpit and pulled out the cloth. I just knew he was going to reveal my actions to God in front of my friends.

But as the cloth was held out for all to see, he said, "Children, what do you see?" I jumped up and said, "There's a spot on the bottom rose." Then all the other children joined in, "I see it, too. Yeah, there's the spot."

Then the preacher gave me the gift of a lifetime. While I no longer remember his name, I do remember what came next. He said, "Look again!" This time we all jumped up and ran to point out the stain. And he responded, "Oh, look at all the beauty you missed by focusing on one very tiny spot. Countless roses in many shades, leaves of green in all shapes and color. Countless hours of time to make the lovely tablecloth, but all you saw and talked about was the one tiny spot. And sometimes we do the same thing with our friends. We only look for the faults and never share the beauty. How sad."

Just as my tablecloth incident left a permanent mark, your early experiences are programmed into your brain with great vigor. The brain is a pattern detector that makes tapes as powerful as your favorite recording. The mind is what we have to use to separate the right from the wrong, the good from the bad, the joy from the sorrow. But if we do not learn to ask ourselves good questions, the old brain tapes rule our lives. If we have one bad experience with an individual from a different culture, part of the world, color of skin or accent, our brain patterns it as fact. No, we do not intend to be or think of ourselves as closed-minded, but it happens to each one of us. We may see powerful images on TV or in the movies, and without our realizing it, that image slips silently into our brains as real.

Our emotions are imprinted in our brains at a very early age. If we do not make a conscious effort, we can close the door to a person who might have become a friend, a co-worker, or a part of our support system. The trick is to keep our minds open, for experience is the master teacher, and an open mind its only hope. For me, "I never met a stranger" means the stereotypes of others will not close the door to new adventures, new friendships, new insights. Bad news sells in our culture, but you don't have to buy it as reality. Think for yourself and the next stranger might just be a great gift to your life.

Career Planning

*Career planning for your generation
is more complex than ever before.
Technology careens
through the best-laid plans.
How do you proceed?*

Career Planning? Not Me

by Gregory DeLucca

Southern Wisconsin was Greg's world until he graduated from the University of Wisconsin. Had he decided to remain in his home town and pursue a "safe" career with a local chemical company, the worlds of soft drinks, wine, food, fashion, farming and international travel would remain unknown quantities. Greg is an example of someone who prepared himself broadly as a businessman, took educated risks, had faith in his capabilities, and let the winds of fortune bring new challenges and opportunities. Greg's essay explains an open-mindedness which has resulted in an exciting life for him and his family — one that has brought associations with the "greats" of the wine, food, fashion, business and political worlds — in his assignments with the Coca-Cola Company, General Electric and entrepreneurial ventures.

Greg now lives in Santa Fe, New Mexico. As he enters the "retired" phase of life, you can be sure he will be open to new adventures.

AFTER ALMOST 40 years of business life, I chuckle to myself about the lofty task that anyone of age 18 and noble mind must diligently pursue — Career Planning. What are you going to do with the rest of your life? Since the expectant longevity of LIFE is now 80-plus years and one's business life is at least 35-plus years, we're talking about doing some real long range planning.

With that said, my nearly 40 business years have been spent in the soft drink, wine, wine capsule manufacturing, industrial synchronous motors, consumer housewares (irons, toasters, fans, electric toothbrushes, etc.) and cryogenic gas industries. In terms of business functions, these many years have been spent as an engineer, product planner, marketing director, operations planner, engineering manager, finance vice president, general manager, president, entrepreneur and purchasing manager.

At age 18, who would have THUNK I would have a Career in Diversity. Was there a plan? Well, maybe. In high school, math and science were my long suits, so I went to college to pursue a chemical engineering degree. With a degree in hand, I went to my first job as a chemical engineer, only to learn that I didn't like solving real life problems as an engineer. I thought, "Maybe I should be a businessman instead." I then returned to Wisconsin to get an MBA. These two degrees have served me well throughout my Career in Diversity. During the MBA program, I came upon my career objective: to become a president or general manager of a business. All of my future job experiences would point me to complementing exposures in order to prepare for my dream job. This plan materialized with my appointment as president of Sterling Vineyards of Napa Valley, California, 20 years later.

The wisdom I would like to share is that it is presumptuous to settle upon a career plan at age 18. How could I ever have forecast a 15 year career in the wine industry? The "pearls" I would like to leave with you are these: be exposed to as many interesting experiences as you can, pick one that will make you passionate in your undertaking, and then do it — and do it well! Then let the winds of time and your desires carry you to the goal that will give you the ultimate joy in your work. Joy in your work should be your career pursuit.

Who knows where that goal will take you. Plan for a Career in Diversity, but don't be confined to a Career Plan.

"Yes, Sir. No Sir. No Excuse, Sir"

by Jim Kimsey

Jim Kimsey founded America Online in 1985. Accumulating piles of money is a common feature of the American dream, and Jim has certainly made that part work. Born into an Irish family of modest means in Washington, DC, he was expelled his senior year from a private Roman Catholic school because he couldn't tolerate the discipline there. Ironically, after a year at Georgetown he accepted an appointment to West Point. When he left the Army, he had $2,000 and a wife and children to support. He stumbled into the restaurant business, used his talent for finding the right people to run things, and recognized the possibilities in the computer world when he received authorization to run stock quotes for the brokers who lunched in his restaurant. Although there were many ups and downs, he extracted himself from his expanded business with a decent profit.

America Online had to break new ground in telecommunications while competing with huge companies. Starting in 1985, AOL kept a low profile, which Jim describes as "a little boat speeding through the bayou," so that the bigger ships couldn't really tell where he was going.

While serving in Viet Nam, Jim became involved with the building of a Catholic orphanage, which he still supports. Deciding to devote the next phase of his life to worthy causes, Jim has turned his attention to the plight of disadvantaged children, and has taken on the challenge of figuring out how technology can help overcome some of the problems in American education. He is embracing a larger societal role with the freedom he has been given, and his impact will be felt in new directions.

MY WEST POINT experience prepared me for life in the following way—I am forever reminded of "Yes, Sir. No, Sir. No excuse, Sir." When I was a cadet, I thought this was unreasonable; there should be explanations. But since then, I've come to understand the true meaning of "no excuse." It simply means that there is no excuse, so don't even think about trying to make one. When you are in battle, it's your job to accomplish your mission and bring your men back alive. There's no excuse if you don't. If you're a business CEO and you don't figure out where the universe is moving or what it takes to make your company successful, there's no excuse. When you have the mindset that there is no excuse, you will be successful.

The Army and my West Point experience taught me the dynamics of leadership and the enormous responsibility you have to look out for the welfare of your people. But I learned that I didn't want to be part of a large organization—that I'd rather do something on my own. Big organizations will always turn on you. It's in their nature; they can't help it. It's nothing to be upset about. You just have to understand the phenomenon. You make arrangements with an individual, but that individual changes his mind, or he's replaced by another person who puts a different perspective on your job. This is the nature of large organizations. It's not an indictment of them; it's simply a statement of fact. It always has been, and always will be. When they roll over in the middle of the night and squash you, they don't do it on purpose. They just forget you are there. That doesn't make you any less dead, but it's something to know in order not to be surprised when it happens.

The danger of making a lot of money is that you equate it with success.

But having a lot of money doesn't necessarily mean that you're successful. It just means that you were lucky. When faced with severe challenges in life, I've made deals with someone upstairs. "If I pass this test, I'll be a better person. If I get through this bankruptcy threat, I'll work for the betterment of mankind." I find that now that I am where I thought I wanted to be, there's this big voice up there saying, "WELL?"

I made a lot of promises, and now it's time to deliver.

Bring Your Heart To Work

by Robin Sheerer

A bright yellow flower looks back at you from Robin's book, **No More Blue Mondays**. This book won the national Ben Franklin award for best career book in 1999, and can be a useful guide as you begin your search for meaningful work. Merging work and happiness is one of Robin's many missions. People who seek her out for career counseling will find themselves looking into their hearts as much or more than looking into their heads. Her newsletter title, "Heart at Work," says it all.

Robin can sort you out quickly. "What are you excited about? When do you feel great about what you are doing?" She will see your strengths in a way you may not have, and she'll catch you on the fears that are holding you back. A normal part of her approach is to stress words such as power and passion, challenging you to take control of your life. Antioch College in Ohio launched Robin into the working world through a program that combines classroom education with life experience. A graduate degree in social group work from the University of Chicago gave her the tools to work in social services with teens, something she did for 13 years prior to creating a career coaching business.

Having lost her own father at 18, Robin has a special understanding of young people and their struggles.

WORK HAS BEEN important to me for as long as I can remember. Throughout my life, if I haven't been able to find a job, I've created one. Because I liked combining work and study, I went to a college that had work as part of the curriculum. By the time I graduated, I had two and one half years of work experience that ranged from nurse's aide to secretary to street gang worker. I have been amazed at how these jobs helped me later in my professional work.

I've learned that a degree is not a career plan. Over the years I've been a social worker, teacher, psychotherapist, consultant, trainer and author. It took me until I was 41 to discover that I love the freedom of working for myself. In my business, I coach people on career and work-related issues. I have worked with people from all walks of life—CEOs to assembly line workers. I have distilled some truths that seem to apply to everyone. Here's my top ten list:

1.   There is no one right way to have a fulfilling work life. Very few people know early in their lives what they want to do, or what they would be best at doing. Give yourself permission to explore jobs and fields.

2.   Pursue what you want to do, not what other people think you should do. The only right work is what's right for you. Don't take a job that doesn't interest you, even if the job is "hot" and pays well. It's too hard to do well if you don't care.

3.   Find a good fit with your interests, talents and skills. Look for a fit rather than a particular job title. The same titles may cover different jobs in different companies.

4.   Network, network, network! Keep in touch with people throughout your whole work life. One way to find a good fit is to network with people who love their work. Find out how they got where they are.

People who love their work are usually generous with advice and help.

5. Work where you are treated well; if you're not, leave. Not all companies are the same; some companies are healthier than others. Don't stay anywhere where you feel victimized.

6. Give time and attention to developing your people skills, as well as technical skills. Take classes, read self-help books and attend workshops. Many jobs require people skills above all others.

7. Design a whole life. Take care of your body and spirit. Poor health or psychological problems can sabotage success at work. If you need therapy, get it.

8. Don't drop your dreams because you hear dire warnings about the economy. All you need is one job.

9. Money isn't everything. Some jobs are worth having regardless of the money. You need to decide how much money you need, not what other people need. From the beginning, start living on less than you make. Sock some money away. Having money in the bank will give you the freedom to make changes.

10. Consider work a gift, not punishment or a war zone. It's the single greatest arena available for you to express yourself, contribute your gifts, and grow and develop as a human being.

It's Not What You Think

by Hart A. Langer

Becoming the top pilot for one of the largest airlines in the world is no small accomplishment. Hart Langer recently retired from United Airlines, having served as senior vice-president for flight operations. Prior to joining United, he served as the chief pilot for Pan American World Airways, where he worked for 21 years.

Hart has a degree in industrial engineering from Pennsylvania State University, served as an instructor pilot in the U.S. Air Force, and then went into commercial aviation. He has served as chairman of the Air Transport Association's Operations Council, as well as chairman of the International Air Transport Association's Technical Committee. The heavy responsibility for moving millions of people through the skies each year requires dedicated people like Hart. One of his co-workers described him as someone who "brings out the best" in those who work for him.

SINCE BEING AN airplane pilot is a very desirable job, I am frequently asked exactly what we at United Airlines are looking for when we hire new pilots. Whenever I speak with groups of high school or college students, they all presume to know the answer—they think we are looking for the most technically proficient pilots we can find. They think we want to hire squadrons of Chuck Yeagers, John Glenns or Steve Canyons. Nothing could be farther from the truth.

In fact, when asked what kind of person we want to hire as a pilot, my response is: "United Airlines wants to hire the same kind of person that you would hire if you were running a family business. We want to hire good employees."

Let me be more specific as to exactly what we want when we hire pilots at United:

We want people who are

1. conscientious,
2. dependable,
3. honest,
4. excellent team players,
5. terrific communicators,
6. "people" people,
7. committed to excellence in everything they do,
8. focused on the customer,
9. outstanding asset managers (someone who can run a $200 million dollar asset—the cost of a 747—in the best interest of the customers and the company),
10. And—by the way—, who happen to be excellent pilots.

You'll notice that of the ten attributes I've listed, only one describes the technical aspects of the job. The rest focus on character traits and what might be called "softer" skills. Here's why:

We have found out over the years that very few airplane accidents are due to a lack of technical proficiency on the part of the pilot. On the contrary, many, many accidents have resulted from a lack of effective communication and teamwork in the cockpit.

Additionally, the world of business today is highly competitive. All companies want to hire people who can really focus on the needs of the paying customer as well as the internal customer, and, therefore, deliver a quality of service that is head and shoulders above that of the competition. So, do not by any means let up on the intensity with which you pursue technical excellence. You really must have it, but it's virtually a given that any employer with whom you interview with will assume you have that. But try--really try— to do some serious soul-searching as to whether your character traits measure up (and if not, what you need to do to improve them). Also, see what you can do to embark on a lifelong program to improve your "people" skills and your communication abilities.

This is the ideal combination, whether it's the airline business or any other business: a technically excellent person with great people skills, who is an outstanding communicator. If you can achieve all of these elements, the sky's the limit!!

"So Tell Me Again What Your Title Is"

by Peri Smilow

The whirlwind that is Peri Smilow is not to be missed if she comes to entertain in your area. She is primarily a singer and songwriter of Jewish music, but not always in conventional ways. She is a cantorial soloist who takes her deep love of her own tradition and crosses over to other cultures — the music of black slavery, a jazz Shabbat, or a project joining with black gospel singers. Rave reviews follow her performances: "I don't think I have ever heard anyone with such a beautiful voice with concurrent masterful guitar skills and originality all woven into one unique package."

Peri can be found using her music to reach inner city kids, the elderly and people from many cultures. The other half of her working life has been spent in Boston and New York in community service programs, including City Year, a popular service-learning program for young volunteers. A graduate of Wesleyan University with a master's degree in educational administration from Harvard, Peri educates us all.

My LIFE AND MY work are one. To the dismay of my beloved mother, I announced when I graduated from college that I didn't want to put on pantyhose to go to work. My working life has been as a non-profit entrepreneur in a series of organizations, some of which I started because there was and is a need.

Sometimes I questioned why inner city kids would want to listen to a suburban Jewish girl from New Jersey who grew up with everything. How could I expect them to believe me when I tell them they can be anybody, when

I know the world can make it hard for them? Still, my heart tells me this is where I belong.

If you want to make a career out of helping others, you have to have a strong personal network to support and teach you. I found a mentor in East Harlem who challenged me. I was a consultant working with his organization and he let me know when I was wrong. I had been accustomed to praise — which I didn't always trust. Believe me, when he took me on it wasn't easy, and it didn't feel great. Through him I learned to seek and trust honest feedback, and to respect people who were straight with me.

I have learned that if you have a non-traditional career, one which confuses your parents, you have to maintain many relationships and be ready to work at any hour. Something in my personality draws me to cross boundaries that will have an impact beyond me. Your family members may not understand this. My mother used to press me for a job title, and at times I had to create one then and there.

Not long ago I faced a serious health crisis, and before I left for the hospital I wrapped myself in the jacket of an organization I started. I said, "I don't think I'm going to die on this operating table, but if I do, I have wrapped myself in something I am proud of." I now know how to put on pantyhose, and you can be darn sure that I do it any time I need to in order to raise money for an organization. If you throw yourself into life with full force, learn all the time, and find people who tell you the truth about yourself, you will grow.

<u>Vision</u>

Having a vision of the future
implies that you can see
a path.
Your next path has
brambles, fog, and forks.
Set off with excitement.

Three Lessons

by David Bomba

When you watch a movie, everything but the acting is a result of the production designer's planning. David had no idea when he was18 years old that he would someday be diving 500 stomach-churning times in a NASA plane to create the weightless scenes in Apollo 13. He was just trying to determine what to do with his drive to be involved somewhere in the design field. His degree in environmental design gave him the background, and his willingness to sacrifice personal comforts to break into a tough business helped him to be in the right place at the right time.

David grew up in New Orleans and attended Texas A & M University. His strong interest in horticulture and gardening combined with architectural training to give David the skills he needed to design outdoor environments for film, and that is how he began to work. He has moved up the movie ranks from art direction to full responsibility for production design. You can see David's name in the credits for "Apollo 13," "Chain Reaction," "My Dog Skip," "Original Sin," and many other films.

Lesson One: READ THE SIGNS

When I was 18, all I knew about my future was that I wanted to be involved in design. I went to Texas A & M because my mother shut my finger in the car door when I was about to visit the other school on my list. Some people receive messages in the form of burning bushes Ouija boards or psychics. Mine came in the form of a throbbing index finger. Ten semesters and one change of major later, I graduated with a degree in environmental design.

Lesson Two: MAKE A DECISION

After that decision has been made, the choice will either present itself as a positive or a negative. Then you will either reward yourself for the good, or you will learn and move on.

My conservative father, a Lutheran minister, delivered his best sermon to me in that very simple statement. When I was vacillating over what to do with my life, he suggested that I quit riding the fence and make some decision. I scraped up $3,000 doing various jobs, placed myself behind the wheel of a VW and headed west to Los Angeles. I had accumulated several loose-leaf pages of names. Names of movies. Names of directors. Names of studios. Names of friends, and friends of friends. My decision was to make an attempt at becoming a motion picture production designer.

Lesson Three: BE PERSISTENT

With over 170 names, I was confident that it wouldn't take long. I dove head first into the very large and very crowded pool of Los Angeles rejection. Getting quite close to my phone list's completion, I came upon a number that I was given by my friend Valerie Karan just days prior to my Houston departure. The name was George Jenkins. I learned that his credits included some of my favorite films such as Klute and Sophie's Choice, and that he had earned an Oscar for All the President's Men. Pushing nerves aside, I dialed the number, gave my name and contact, and asked for a meeting. George's silence was followed by my repetition of Valerie's name. More silence. I waited for the all-too-familiar "click." Great thanks to fate, there was no click. George kindly obliged my questions and invited me to audit a class on production design that he was teaching at UCLA. In the meantime, I showed up on sets in case someone else hadn't, lived in a cubicle and sold carpeting out of a van, and survived with a stint behind the counter at a drycleaner. When my sister Beth, a flight attendant, came to town, I had an actual meal.

Sixteen years in the film industry have taken me to many unique and wonderful places. They vary in interest and stomach-upsetting degrees, from NASA's KC-135 "Vomit Comet" (used for filming weightless scenes in Apollo 13), to the 30-plus-mile-long and quarter mile deep Chicago Drainage Tunnel, to the beautiful solitude of Gallinas Canyon, New Mexico — constant challenges, constant invention, constant puzzles.

Read the signs, make a decision and persevere.

You Have to Dream

by Jody Lynn Titus

> If you love what you do, you will never work
> another day in your life." ~*Confucius*.

"Jody, your life is at the very least a 'made for TV' movie. Keep a journal," I used to say. In my years as a counselor, Jody stands out as a fighter with grit. Bone cancer struck when Jody was tenth grade, in the midst of her family breaking apart in an acrimonious divorce. She had always been in fast-track classes, but now tried to do her high school work from a horizontal position as she struggled with the effects of chemotherapy. Moving to live with one parent and then the other, she was far behind her peers in high school. Jody was 18 and trying to decide what to do about school when she started to work through a college counseling program for students who have faced cancer. Spike Gummere, the director of admissions at Lake Forest College, advised Jody to forget about high school and suggested that she start at the community college and earn her way to full status at Lake Forest.

Jody did this in an incredible fashion. She started college, maintaining herself by working in a pharmacy by day and a service station by night — all with a fused right wrist which required a brace. When her first grades were at the top, she moved to Lake Forest as a chemistry major. Jody found the right mentor, Dr. William Martin, who allowed her to double up on classes, attended events with her when she received awards and guided her to catch up with her peers when others did not believe it would be possible.

Jody graduated Magna Cum Laude with Honors in Chemistry and in Senior Thesis. She is a member of Phi Beta Kappa and Sigma Xi, and went on to graduate school in Synthetic Organic Chemistry at the University of California-Irvine. When you are having a bad day, you might think of Jody and her determination.

Many of us spend so much time learning to be team players and to be successful with group interactions that we accept what we believe others think of us and expect us to become. We need to dream — to have a dream about what we want to be and do, regardless of what others think. To find out about our individual selves, we need to get out and have new experiences.

Do not place limitations on your abilities or fear initial failures because you can stop your forward progress before you have given yourself a real chance. No one else can really tell you who you are and you cannot be afraid to challenge yourself to find out. Initially, I wanted to be a medical doctor since I had seen so much hospital time in my life and had witnessed so many events on the health care scene, both positive and negative. However, while in college, I discovered that the chance to cure illness on the molecular level proved to be much more fascinating.

My academic research is multi-faceted, but has as its single goal a better understanding of the central nervous system. Spending my time designing molecules to use as probes in investigating the glutamate transmitter system is a far cry from time spent during those days of treatment when I wondered if I would even finish high school. What I am doing may some day benefit people with learning and memory problems, be they stroke or Alzheimer's patients.

Your dream may require lots of effort because most of us are not born with all of the knowledge and experience needed to achieve our dreams. Your dream may require sacrifices. However, remember that anything worthwhile (especially you) always does. Besides, at least later in life you will not be plagued with wondering, "What if...?"

You will have already given yourself the answers.

Leadership

Governor Angus King, Jr.

If you call the Governor's Office in Maine, Angus King may answer his own phone. He is the people's governor, an Independent who stands between the Republicans and Democrats. If you are a politician, this is often an awkward place to be with no one to catch you, as both sides may try to tip you over. Obviously, he took his own advice when he decided to run as an Independent because that is — in political terms — taking an enormous chance. He was not only elected; he's been re-elected.

Governor King was born in Virginia, attended Dartmouth College and the University of Virginia Law School, and began his law career in legal assistance in Skowhegan, Maine. In 1972, he became Chief Counsel to the U.S. Senate Subcommittee on Alcoholism and Narcotics in Washington, D.C. He returned to his adopted state and began to host a public television show called "Maine Watch." Governor King has a background in alternative energy development and is well equipped to lead his state, which remains rich in natural resources and has not yet succumbed to over-development. Rumor has it that Governor King likes nothing better than to take off on his Harley-Davidson motorcycle.

I'VE FIGURED OUT what leadership is all about. It only took me five years as governor and some pretty serious ups and downs, but I've arrived at a working definition of what this mysterious thing—which is so important to any enterprise—is all about.

Here are the three elements:

1. The ability to visualize the future. Vision is the usual shorthand term, but what it really means is the ability to see what the future is likely to look like, not necessarily next week, but five, ten, twenty years out. For example, based upon your knowledge of caterpillars and the thickness of a bears' fur, some time in late August you know it's going to be a cold winter.

2. The ability to figure out what that future will require of your organization, tribe, state, nation, club or you. To continue the example, you next know that you'll soon need an extra supply of warm blankets and more corn than usual.

3. (This is the hard part.) The ability to move the organization to take the necessary steps to cope with the future. In other words, stop dancing and plant that corn.

This is the essential role of the leader in any organization. The challenge in most cases is to have the discipline to detach from the day-to-days and think about the future, to discern what's coming or, perhaps more importantly, what could be coming if you play your cards right. This is vision—the ability to understand the present and see where it leads, and then to see alternative futures which may be influenced by what we do in the here and now.

The middle part is easier—once you get a fix on the likely future, what you have to do to prepare is usually pretty clear. If you're running Coca-Cola and you see that people are moving toward healthier lifestyles, it's pretty clear you should get into the juice business, sooner rather than later.

As noted above, the hardest part is then getting the group to buy into both your vision and your prescription. Change in any human institution is never easy (one of my fellow governors says "everyone's for progress, no one's for change") and there are always ten reasons not to do things differently. The challenge is to devise the right strategy for the circumstances.

That strategy at this stage can take many forms—edict, if you're fortunate enough to be the dictator, leverage based upon some kind of institutional power (I'll veto the bill unless XYZ is included"), but more usually consists of some combination of persuasion, cajolery, and persistence. The final factor to tip the balance is being right—awakening in your followers what might have been an unconscious knowledge that yes, it does look like it might be cold this winter and yes, I guess we'd better get ready.

And if you're really lucky, you'll make it through the winter to direct the flood control efforts come Spring.

Working

by Bernie Sahlins

Your parents can't imagine Saturday Night Live without John Belushi, Gilda Radner and Martin Short, or Ghostbusters without Harold Ramis and Bill Murray. But we wouldn't have those memories without Bernie Sahlins, the co-founder, producer, and director of The Second City. One hundred fifty chairs bought at auction for a dollar apiece held the audience for an experiment in theater in a modest Chicago neighborhood back in 1959. The Second City took off, and is still a popular entertainment destination in both Chicago and Toronto.

Bernie set the standard for the training of some of the best comedy talents working today. Players at The Second City must develop their own material and fine-tune it with the audiences who stay for the free improvisational sessions after the show. Good comedy requires that the performers learn Bernie's lessons to respect the intelligence of the audience, and give 100% of themselves, while challenging their own intellects.

A graduate of the University of Chicago, Bernie writes, directs, translates, and produces for TV, radio, the stage, and film. He has won numerous awards for innovation in theater. His autobiography, *Days and Nights at the Second City*, tells his story.

WHEN IT COMES to work, to the activity you will spend your days doing, you have a choice. Take a nine to five job that might pay well but is just a job or find a calling—a vocation—that does not create a separation between your life and your work. I will use the example of a life in the theater because that has been my own vocation.

Working in the theater is attractive to so many people because it is a place of commitment. Everyone in the theater has a goal outside immediate wants and needs: to serve the work, to create something beautiful.

If you do decide to work in this field, though you may be primarily interested in acting or directing, it is important to learn to do all the jobs in a theater—stage management, lighting, costume and scene design. You are then more likely to find work in what is a crowded field.

There are no lowly jobs in the theater. A dramatic production is a great leveler. A person may come to the work as a star and leave as a star, but during the production all who work are equal. Nor does it matter if you wind up working in a storefront theater or a huge professional enterprise. The commitment and satisfactions are the same. What's more, in all theaters you will find yourself working at the highest level of your skills and intelligence.

What does it mean to work like this? Pride, satisfaction and the knowledge that you, along with others, served a worthy cause. You will make deep, long-lasting friendships and you will be constantly challenged.

I have dwelt on the theater because that is my own commitment. But there are many routes to such commitment: from social work to foundations, from museum work to medicine. The principles are the same. Find something to which you can commit. Learn all of its facets and keep learning every day. Challenge yourself. When you find yourself in a job where you have stopped learning, leave it. Set your goals at the highest level: president, publisher, professor. You may not reach it, but the striving makes the life. Seek your vocation.

Mentors

You may be able to shortcut the path
To wisdom
By finding seasoned, caring people to help you on the way.
In a complex world, you may fear to
ask for help.
Many people find deep satisfaction
in teaching you what they know.

Bernstein and Me

by Jerry Hadley

As a little boy, Jerry sat on his Italian grandfather's lap and absorbed the radio broadcasts of the Metropolitan Opera. The first time he stepped on that stage as a performer had to give him an amazing feeling. Now a world class opera star, Jerry grew up on an Illinois farm where there were no talent scouts to hear his tenor voice ringing over the rumble of the tractor.

Bradley University gave him a vocal start, and he met his wife, Cheryl Drake, during his master's studies at the University of Illinois. Cheryl is a superb pianist who accompanies him in his recitals. Beverly Sills brought him to the New York City Opera, where in his first performance, inadvertently the feathers in his hat caught on fire. When Paul McCartney called and asked Jerry to sing Paul's autobiographical part in the premier performance of the Liverpool Oratorio, Jerry's "inner teenager" had to pinch himself.

Jerry has appeared on all the major opera stages of the world, has a lengthy list of recordings and Grammy awards, and continues to do innovative work. In 1999, he premiered the title role in the opera The Great Gatsby at the Metropolitan Opera. As a student of history and languages, he performs Neapolitan folk songs along with the usual operatic languages, and in his recitals, features Carl Sandburg's poetry set to music. He remains a warm, witty and joyfully enthusiastic person. When Jerry was 18, he could not have imagined the scope of his future career.

IT WAS MY great pleasure to know and work with the legendary Leonard Bernstein. I have rubbed shoulders with lots of giants of my profession, but

Lenny was very special. I don't think it is an exaggeration to say that he changed my life.

He was for most Americans a cultural icon and a larger-than-life personality. I remember him as the man who "invented" music for me. Having grown up on a farm in central Illinois, I did not have access to the great concert halls and opera houses. I was musically inclined, and was fortunate to have Italian immigrant relatives on my mother's side of the family who encouraged those embryonic impulses, but it was Lenny and the "Young People's Concerts" (in glorious black and white)on CBS television on Sunday afternoons that opened my eyes to the wonders of the world of music.

When I finally met and started working with Lenny, I found out that the man I had seen on the TV screen was very much flesh and blood as well. Here was the man who not only wrote West Side Story — one of the pillars of the central canon of the American musical theater — and hundreds of other works; he was also one of the two or three greatest conductors of his generation, a virtuosic pianist, a scholar and teacher with few equals, and the man who single-handedly resurrected the works of Gustav Mahler and secured that composer's legacy for our time. There I was, a hard-working and somewhat self-conscious, but eager young singer with the scent of the farm still lingering on the soles of my shoes. Yet, miraculously, it didn't matter to Lenny from whence I had come. He was interested only in the potential of the human spirit to fly beyond its self-imposed bounds.

Lenny introduced me to a world without fear. He never saw limitations, only possibilities. I remember standing on stage and looking into his eyes as he stood on the podium, believing in those moments that neither were the gates of hell unassailable nor the gates of heaven unattainable. He took all of us who performed with him to places we scarcely dreamed we could go. He taught us to do our homework, to prepare and study and work, and to take nothing for granted; then he taught us to fly.

I remember one rehearsal in particular. Three other singers and I had just sung for Lenny the "Benedictus" from the Mozart Requiem in preparation for upcoming performances and a recording. We were very focused, intense and perfect. When we finished, Lenny threw down his baton and said, "That really sucked!" As you can imagine, we were all aghast and upset that we had not pleased him — particularly when we knew that we had crossed all the "t"s and dotted all the "i"s, and had performed the piece "perfectly". He looked at us, smiled and said, "Dammit, kids, don't you realize that your intelligence and preparation will NEVER leave you if you have the courage to engage your hearts? Let'em know what YOU think and feel, but do it THROUGH what the guy wrote on the page!"

We already knew that, but we were intent on "pleasing the teacher," on figuratively getting a good grade. What Lenny advocated and lived was to take responsibility for one's actions, to know why one does what one does, to do nothing without preparation, but to be willing to embrace the serendipity of the moment — in short, to be all of who one is! That never meant for him to "do one's own thing" at the expense of others, nor to approach a task with arrogance bred by ignorance and ill-preparedness.

Lenny was the most well read, most studious, most thoughtful, best prepared and most technically schooled musician I have ever met. He was also the most fearless, fun-loving, generous and incredibly child-like spirit I have ever known. The former qualities enabled him to display the latter without reservation. He was a life force. His great and transcendent qualities (magnified greatly by his huge personality) were balanced by the human foibles that we all have so that he was a fully-realized human being.

His extraordinary talents and God-given unique personal qualities notwithstanding, Lenny was also my friend. I loved him like a father, brother and playmate all rolled into one. His enduring legacy to me is the belief that we are bound only by our fear and our unwillingness to love. Lenny loved life, and he loved making music. He loved learning. He loved to share the things he loved with others, and his infectious effusiveness turned his performances into collective musical and emotional lovefests. Learning and growth cannot take place in an atmosphere of fear and arrogance, whereas love can indeed conquer all.

Thanks, Lenny. We all miss you.

Point to the Passer

by Dean Smith

Students at the University of North Carolina now cheer their basketball team from the Dean E. Smith Center, also known as "The Dean Dome." The most successful college coach in basketball history, Dean Smith has guided players not only in the fine points of the game, but also in the fine points of life.

Dean was raised in Emporia, Kansas, the son of a coach and a teacher who raised him with strong religious values. His book, *A Coach's Life*, pays tribute to that upbringing. He recalls the determination of his highly educated mother, who insisted that her children read a book a week. "My parents were determined that we see every person as valuable, unique, and particular—and equal before our Creator."

A serious athlete himself, Dean went on to play basketball and baseball at the University of Kansas. Families like Dean's may be hard to find these days, but his life as a leader and mentor of young men, Michael Jordan among them, teaches us what happens when you take all of your responsibilities and match them with your beliefs.

THE MENTORING of my players as they worked to perfect the game of basketball has been my professional life. No game requires more teamwork; one's mistakes are immediately evident, and time can be your friend or your enemy. You may not play basketball, but you have probably watched it. As a player, I had to learn from my own father and my college coach; then I learned my craft from coaches under whom I worked. Lessons from all of them were incorporated into the way we developed the program at North Carolina.

The importance of ritual in building a culture became evident to me as we began building the subtle lessons of life into the way we trained our teams. Just as families build unique identities through holiday rituals, as well as the seemingly hard and fast rules of family life and discipline, team solidarity depends upon shared experiences and customs which enhance the experience for everyone and make them feel a special part of events.

One of the most important rituals that we developed at North Carolina was the custom of "point to the passer." Everyone watching a game can tell you who just scored, but can they tell you who gave up the ball to a player who might be in a better position to score? This ritual began by asking the scorer to thank the person with a small gesture, but grew on its own to encompass the bench, the coaches, and even at times the crowd. When the passer acts for the good of the overall effort and sacrifices his own chance to shoot, our entire bench jumps up and points to the passer. Unselfish play is the foundation of teamwork.

I like to think that this small gesture makes an impact beyond the game itself. Unselfishness and sacrifice for the good of a larger effort characterize important events in history, and recognizing those people who quietly make a difference is a quality found in leaders who get the most from their subordinates.

Learning to work effectively with others takes practice, lots of it. Sometimes you won't feel appreciated or recognized, but if you consistently acknowledge the assistance you receive from others, and "point to the passer," your leadership skills will grow, and that respect you show to a fellow human being will be returned to you in full measure.

The Power Of Doughnuts

by Debra Daniel

Flush a toilet in Cut and Shoot, Texas, and you have Debra Daniel to thank. Her company, DEI Construction, laid the 43 miles of water lines required to give the town a new water system.

Debra started out as an ambitious young woman doing shift work at Exxon. She soon tired of that and began selling building materials for road building and other large construction projects—everything from nuts and bolts to chemicals. She eventually became involved in rewriting the specifications for building materials to be used in the city of Houston. With that knowledge and a drive to be on her own, she took a chance on becoming the owner of a construction company in a highly male-dominated world. She credits a certain amount of inner toughness to the fact that her brothers once attempted to throw her off the roof with balloons and an umbrella to see if she would float.

If Debra doesn't know something, she's quick to look for someone to teach her. She is bursting with energy, popular with her employees, and feels quite at home in her boots and hard hat.

I STILL CALL HIM Uncle Jack. It was about 20 years ago that I was terrified of being seen as a bimbo who didn't belong in a man's business. I searched for someone to be my mentor — someone who would be objective. Jack Glasgow was VP of a large construction company. He agreed to help me learn the business if I would come in early in the morning before the work day began.

Since I was working on commission selling construction materials, I couldn't afford fancy lunches. So I got up early, bought fresh donuts and headed for Jack's office. That was the beginning. I bought the donuts; he made the coffee and taught me. He taught me about my competition, the laboratory tests for materials, how to manage the workers and what to watch out for. When I had learned enough to start my own business, Uncle Jack even came to work for me for a few months.

My first office was my dining room; a door topping two filing cabinets was my desk. I took my last two paychecks and ran scared the whole first year. My car was a clunker which I hoped would hold up for six months. I had dealt with trucking companies in my other job and was able to find a little old man who owned 20 trucks, but was using only eight of them. By the end of the first year, he had earned $450,000 and we were both on our way.

The bimbo thing didn't go away easily. Men hit on me all the time, and once I had to deck a guy. Now it's less of a problem because I've added a hundred pounds to my frame. There's nothing fragile about me, especially when I'm wearing my hard hat.

Once you find your mentor in work that you love, you can leap ahead of the competition because all that knowledge piles onto your own experience. For me, there's no better rush than closing a sale that started with a cold call. I've switched from donuts to cookies now. My car trunk is full of cookies in tins. I give them to the receptionist, who never forgets me after that. Plenty of people wine and dine "the big guys," but if you are good to their help, it pays off in a big way.

Without Uncle Jack, I still might have made it on my own, but I hate to think about it.

Money

You have to come to terms with it.

Be Ready to Sweat

by Gary Dahl

At the time the Pet Rock craze hit the nation, Gary Dahl was asked on national television if he felt guilty charging $5 for a rock. His answer "—— no" was bleeped out, but why shouldn't people be rewarded for their innovations? Gary was born in North Dakota and grew up in the Pacific Northwest. He served in the Marine Corps for three years, then attended Washington State University. He studied hotel and restaurant management, but immediately went into advertising. He still loves to cook and does so with the best of them. He admits that once the pet rock made him rich, he never looked back, and now claims that his swimming pool is bigger than the home he and his wife, Marguerite, were living in when the pet rock took off.

Gary runs his own company, Gary Dahl Creative Services, in San Jose, California. His agency specializes in broadcast advertising. He obviously has a terrific time in his chosen field.

Innovators are people who think in divergent ways. Gary's creative mind was able to grasp the possibilities of his idea, and his ability to follow through made the difference. The next time you see a simple notion making money for its creator and catch yourself saying, "Ow! Why didn't I think of that?" remember that the simple item you see before you represents hard work and divergent thinking. Open your own mind to your next offbeat idea, and see how it flies.

THE DAY I first uttered the words, "pet rock," I was enjoying a peaceful evening with friends in a saloon in Los Gatos, California. The conversation had turned to the cost of keeping animals. Out of the blue I said that I didn't have to worry about that because I had a pet rock. Everyone laughed when I described how well it would "stay" on command.

At the time, I was working as a creative director to introduce new products to the marketplace. The fact that I was dead broke was a problem, but the idea became an obsession. I thought first of a spoof of a dog training manual, bringing it out as a book. I worked on it every spare minute and it was a hoot. As I researched book publishers and distributors, I realized that making a success of the idea as a book would be extremely difficult. Then it hit me. I would package "The Official Pet Rock Training Manual" with an actual rock so that I could skip bookstores and put the whole enchilada into gift and stationery stores.

My wife, Marguerite, and I scoured the beach in Santa Cruz for the prototypical pet rock. I still have the original—as plain an egg-shaped beach pebble as there ever was. Patrick Welch, a graphic designer, also had a demented sense of humor and he designed the "pet rock" carrying case. A friend gave me a sliver of space at the San Francisco Gift Show and the Pet Rock was a smash. We took orders for thousands. The problem was that I didn't have thousands, and I definitely didn't have the money to get them.

I went into a bank and asked for money to finance a pet rock. I quickly learned a lesson that has stuck with me since: you can borrow money from a bank only when you can prove, beyond a shadow of a doubt, that you don't really need it. Finally with a pile of orders, I was able to convince a former employer to share in the venture. So the pet rock became part of the country's cultural history—the fad of the year.

A publisher once asked me to write a "self help" book. I walked away from it. I did not then, nor do I now, feel qualified to offer self help advice to anyone. Suffice it to say that all the trite statements are true: If you have an idea that you truly feel will be successful, you must remain totally focused on it and be willing to make many sacrifices to see it through to conclusion. Win or lose, it's a lot of damn work.

Preparation and Execution

by Vasco McCoy

Vasco McCoy was born in Texarkana, Texas, and 70-some years later, still lives there. He was educated at Culver Military Academy and Harvard College. Certain that he did not want to work in the family dress shop, he went to Canada to begin an investment career. There he met his wife, Pamela, and returned to his hometown to establish himself as a stockbroker. His essay reveals the path he took to become financially successful.

As a result, he was able to finance a chair at Harvard College which is devoted to the study of the upper stratosphere, i.e. the ozone layer. Always maintaining a consuming interest in learning, Vasco was appointed to Harvard's Visiting Committee for East Asian Studies and the Visiting Committee of the Peabody Museum.

Vasco is an inveterate traveler. In the last 35 years, he and his wife have visited over 100 countries. He enjoys nature photography and has photographed travelers' delights from ritual ceremonies in New Guinea to the wandering albatross near the Antarctic. Vasco is an example of someone who is always learning. His formal education gave him the background, but finding the theories of one man gave him freedom.

IT'S NEVER too late to start a new endeavor, change the course of your life, or to broaden your experience and discover. A principle I learned first in an academic sense is that in the relationship between preparation and execution, before we can accomplish something, we must prepare ourselves.

During a period of preparation, we go through what is often a difficult apprenticeship — a period of trial and error. Finally, we learn the skills it takes to do whatever is our ambition to accomplish. Not that all or even some of our aspirations can be accomplished. Finding our true potential is also part of life, but my point is the need to arrive at a long-term goal. Achievement and success are possible only after a period of preparation. Yet, while you are in that period of preparation, you cannot begin to understand the consequences of "execution" that will later alter your life.

I don't mean to preach, but as an illustration let me suggest something that most—if not all—young people face. Are you going to smoke? As a teenager, I decided to begin smoking cigarettes. I smoked one or two packs, only to discover I didn't like the sensation; I've never smoked since. As I turned 70, I discovered that several of my friends died of lung cancer or other illnesses brought on by smoking. What seemed innocent enough as a youth had profound consequences later. When you become addicted to nicotine as a teenager, you can't possibly know what it will be like to be 60 and in poor health. Yet, those consequences of actions happen every day.

Let's move to a more positive note. When I was in my 20s, I began to read a steady stream of books and magazines about the stock market. In my 40s, I began to speculate in commodities, starting with cocoa. Within six months, I was in the midst of losing a fourth of all my capital. I stuck with my efforts and was rewarded with a market that went up to the point where I multiplied my capital several times. However, I didn't really know what I was doing. Then I took a correspondence course that taught me how to analyze the markets in terms of preparation (horizontal moves) and execution (sharp fast moves up or down). If you study a chart showing the history of a stock move, you will spot the period of preparation. From this education, I have enjoyed many experiences wherein I have learned to anticipate and understand better the concepts of preparation and execution.

I have not been afraid to fail. Wanting to do something doesn't mean you will be able to succeed, but setting your long-term goals based upon an understanding of your own talents and abilities is worthwhile. First, you go through a long period of preparation and then a relatively short period of execution where you pull all of the learning together to achieve your goal. This may sound abstract and remote, but I really believe it is a fundamental part of life. The impatience of youth may cause you to move before you are fully prepared. Always ask yourself if there is anything else you could learn about something before you make your move.

When Will You Start?

by Paula Sestito

A Junior Year Abroad program is a common experience for U.S. college students. In case anyone questions its value in your case, point to Paula's career path. Paula was a nineteen year-old student at Loyola University in Chicago when she went to Rome to study and improve her Italian. Without that year, she may never have landed that first job as an export manager in Florence, which she describes as "ten carefree years" learning about international trade in a city she loved.

Working in Chicago for the Banco di Roma brought her into the larger world of international banking. Paula seizes opportunities when they present themselves, knowing that she can always learn what she has to know about a new situation. As a vice president of Citibank, she has lived in Milan and London, where she has worked with financial strategies involving more than a hundred emerging market countries. Whether checking out a site for a dam in Ethiopia or determining the feasibility of a tire manufacturing plant in Brazil, Paula brings her experience to bear. Her son Joel is following his mother's example, and is a freshly minted international lawyer who also spent a study abroad term in Florence.

DURING MY TWENTIES, while I was working in Italy, I decided that I didn't earn enough money to put anything into savings. I didn't think I needed to start saving so early for future needs, so I procrastinated further. If I had started saving just $20 per month, today I would have accumulated almost $50,000 (assuming an 8% annual rate of return.) The power of compounding money can have dramatic results, especially if you start early. If you can manage today to save $2,000 a year (only $38.50 a week) at an average annual return of 8%, you can end up with almost one million dollars by the time you are 65 years old as indicated on the attached table. No matter what you're earning today, you should try to develop good savings habits now.

How do you get started? As with anything new, you need to keep at it. Be persistent. Once you see results. saving will become easier.

1. Start saving early: The key to success is how long you save, not how much. The results of compounding money over time are impressive.
2. Make saving a habit: If possible you should set up automatic deposits. You can't spend money you never see. If you are working, you might be able to have money automatically withdrawn from your paycheck.
3. Set realistic goals: Be sure to set goals you can meet. If you can only manage $20 per month, don't try to save $75. As your income increases, you can adjust your savings accordingly.
4. Keep it simple: Only invest in financial instruments you understand. It is now possible ,to buy a few shares of a growth company at a time through discount brokers. Pass up buying the fancy ski jacket and turn it into a few shares of your favorite ski jacket company. Learn about growth opportunities.
5. Save extra money: Any cash gifts, bonuses or tax refunds should go straight into savings. What's important is to start saving now. This is the best time in your life to begin saving and compounding your money!

COMPOUNDING YOUR MONEY					
Age	Annual Investment	Cumulative Value	Annual Investment	Cumulative Value	Annual Investment	Cumulative Value
18	$2,000	$2,000			$2,000	$2,000
19	$2,000	$4,160			$2,000	$4,160
20	$2,000	$6,493			$2,000	$6,493
21	$2,000	$9,012			$2,000	$9,012
22	$2,000	$11,733			$2,000	$11,733
23	$2,000	$14,672			$2,000	$14,672
24	$2,000	$17,846			$2,000	$17,846
25	$2,000	$21,273			$2,000	$21,273
26	$2,000	$24,975			$2,000	$24,975
27	$2,000	$28,973			$2,000	$28,973
28	none	$31,291	$2,000	$2,000	$2,000	$33,291
29	none	$33,794	continue	$4,160	continue	$37,954
.		.	.	.		.
.		.	.	.		.
65	none	$539,632	$2,000	$440,632	$2,000	$980,264
Total	$20,000	$539,632	$76,000	$440,632	$96,000	$980,264

Using Your Intellect

You have the best computer
in your own head.
Its capacity expands
with use.

Sherlock of the Forest

by Jane Bock

Jane is a modern day detective who has contributed to the emerging field of forensic botany. She comes from a powerful line of intellectual women, all as only children. It was very unusual for women of Jane's great grandmother's time to attend college, but she began a tradition of teaching which continues unbroken through five generations that include Jane's daughter, Laura.

Growing up in rural northern Indiana, Jane was surrounded by a culture where a common knowledge of plants and plant life was important. Her three degrees in botany come from Duke University (undergraduate), Indiana University (master's) and the University of California at Berkeley (Ph.D). Her distinguished career has yielded many honors. She is on the board of trustees of the Colorado Nature Conservancy, was named a Charles A. Lindbergh Fellow and has received commendations from the Colorado Bureau of Investigation and the Colorado Coroners Association. Her many academic publications range from the study of vegetation in the Caucasus to an article which discussed pests, poisons, and pot.

Jane has a taught a range of botany courses at the University of Colorado and credits the encouragement and collaboration of her colleague, David Norris, for stretching their possibilities beyond anything they ever expected.

THE TOPPINGS ON a pizza once helped me contribute to the solution of a murder case. Would I have believed when I was calmly studying botany at three universities that it would lead me to anlayzing hidden gravesites and working with police investigations around the world?

Students who see themselves as non-scientists often avoid what they perceive as the drudgery of introductory science courses, assuming that this knowledge is not relevant to their futures. In my experience, the solution to a problem may depend upon the knowledge gained in a surprising variety of disciplines. For example, Necrosearch International, a non-profit group which I helped found, searches for clandestine graves in and outside of the United States. A recent scout team consisted of search dogs and their handler, along with an expert in ground-penetrating radar. Another scout team consisted of two anthropologists and a botanist. We have required the services of a zoologist, an aerial photographer and a psychiatrist. All of these fields have their own academic rigors, and the well-trained mind knows enough about all the others to recognize when ideas and facts merge to strengthen evidence.

One of our most satisfying cases began when a clump of human hair entangled with conifer needles was turned in to the Gunnison County, Colorado, sheriff's office.

Using DNA techniques, the hair was matched to a hairbrush which had belonged to a young woman who disappeared 17 years earlier. Her suspected killer had gone free because the body had never been found. It became my task to identify the likely elevation in which that particular conifer grew. Based upon my findings, the grave was located and her killer was convicted.

Sunflowers assisted me in determining the timing of a death. The victim had been hidden in a ditch and covered with them. By pulling up fresh sunflowers and observing their rate of wilting and decomposition, I was able to establish the likely time of death and a conviction followed.

It never occurred to me that I would become a botanical detective when I followed my love of plants into a scientific career. When a pathologist affiliated with the Denver Coroner's office called to ask if I would help identify some vegetable content from a victim's stomach, I discovered that this intriguing project had no body of literature to help, but I was excited by the challenge. Back to the basic textbooks and clues of cell configuration; beans, cabbage and green peppers had left their mark. The fact that the victim had a recent meal, probably with her assailant, indicated that he was known to her.

Arthur Conan Doyle combined literature and science to give us Sherlock Holmes.

My microscope and curiosity have added immeasurable richness to my life as part of a group of scientific detectives. Louis Pasteur stated, "Chance favors the prepared mind." The preparation may seem endless to a young person, but the rewards are great.

The Record

by Wendell Berry

Wendell Berry is a farmer. He is also a poet, a novelist, and a critic of the path on which industrialization has led us. Some years ago, he wrote a widely quoted essay about why he will never have a computer. Ironically, if you put his name into a web search on your computer, it surfaces hundreds of times. College students headline their personal web pages with his quotes and poems; professors assign his writings to philosophy, English and political science classes. Prominent magazines feature his articles, which challenge us to slow down and care for the land and one another.

Wendell still farms in his ancestral community in Kentucky. Poems grow from his interaction with the cycles of nature, and from his connection to the people of his community. His essays lament the loss of personal closeness and the rise of material gain in today's society, and his novels explore the richness of human relationships. As a young writer, a year after graduation from the University of Kentucky, he was selected as a fellow in Wallace Stegner's prestigious writing workshop at Stanford University. Finding the right mentor in his formative years as a writer, he has formed a striking marriage between the precision of his words and the ruminations of his heart.

The Record

My old friend tells us how the country changed:
where the grist mill was on Cane Run,
now gone; where the peach orchard was,

gone too; where the Springport Road was, gone
beneath returning trees; how the creek ran three weeks
after a good rain, long ago, no more;
how when these hillsides first were plowed, the soil
was black and deep, no stones, and that was long ago;
where the wild turkeys roosted in the old days;
"You'd have to know this country mighty well
before I could tell you where."

And my young friend says: "Have him speak this
into a recorder. It is precious. It should be saved."
I know the panic of that wish to save
the vital knowledge of the old times, handed down,
for it is rising off the earth, fraying away
in the wind and the coming day.
As the machines come and the people go
the old names rise, chattering, and depart.

But knowledge of my own going into old time
tells me no. Because it must be saved,
do not tell it to a machine to save it.
That old man speaking you have heard
since your boyhood, since his prime, his voice
speaking out of lives long dead, their minds
speaking in his own, by winter fires, in fields and woods,

in barns while rain beat on the roofs
and wind shook the girders. Stay and listen
until he dies or you die, for death
is in this, and grief is in it. Live here
as one who knows these things. Stay, if you live;
listen and answer. Listen to the next one
like him, if there is to be one. Be
the next one like him, if you must;
stay and wait. Tell your children. Tell them
to tell their children. As you depart
toward the coming light, turn back
and speak, as the creek steps downward
over the rocks, saying the same changing thing
in the same place as it goes.

When the record is made, the unchanging
word carried to a safe place
in a time not here, the assemblage
of minds dead and living, the loved lineage
dispersed, silent, turned away, the dead
dead at last, it will be too late.

Find Your Principles

by Edwin J. Blosser

The Amish came to America from Europe in the 18th and19th centuries because of their religious beliefs. They have been allowed to maintain their stance as pacifists and farmers, providing their own education for their children. When you walk into the pristine office of Midwest Bio-Systems, you will sense a constant hum of purposeful activity from the Amish folk who are dealing with customers from California to Canada to Florida. A magazine rack holds obscure titles: *Biocycle*, *Waste News*, *Resource Recycling*. Edwin is back home from his travels, perhaps from Australia, or from speaking at a conference filled with academics and environmentalists. His story proves that you can educate yourself without formal training or degrees, and people will take you seriously.

Municipalities all over America are digesting their refuse into viable compost in months instead of years because of the products and methods employed by Midwest Bio-Systems. Farmers are producing more and better food. People are surprised to learn that an Amish man speaks at meetings and does constant research and teaching, while also living fully in his religious community. The research goes on, and the mission continues.

I BELIEVE IN CREATION. God set this creation in order and the principles haven't varied. Cause and effect in nature is perfect. We just have to learn how to optimize our gifts and set our course on principles. I want to tell you how that has worked in my life. My nature is gung-ho or not at all. The Amish always want to know the workings of a matter. We want to be responsible with our money, which is a gift from God, and not spend frivolously.

When I was 20, my father-in-law sent me to a seminar on renewable agriculture. At that moment I found my path. I was positive 100% within my soul I was dealing with the process God created and means for us to apply. But I had to learn how to work with it. I had failures and disheartenments, but I knew the vision wasn't wrong. If I made a failure, I knew I was on the right path taking the wrong fork. You're always centering yourself. An airplane is never exactly on course, but centers itself on the beacon, always correcting.

The mentors I had made all the difference. My father's logical mind, and my father-in-law's encouragement and patience started me out. At the time, farmers were being taught that chemicals were the way to go. But that leads to nutrient tie-up and does not renew the soil. I found a man in Minnesota, Dr. Dan Skow, who was willing to tutor me. Five months of the year for three years I studied chemistry and soil agronomy intensely. I studied the work of great scientists and began putting it together in a practical way. I tried out experiments on my father-in-law's farm. He was very patient with me as I tried things that didn't work. Finally results became positive and I began to consult on soil health with a few clients.

Then I met a wonderful man named Dave Larson who had a mission and vision of how God intended this plant growing business to be. I got really excited because we had such a synergistic relationship. We had the trip of our lives visiting Dr. Siegfried Luebke in Austria, learning from his research on enzymes and plant life and how to produce the most nutritious food. We continued to experiment with liquid biologicals until we feel that we now have the best product in America to make living soil. Although Dave died in 1996, our work together lives on.

You may not think that soil is anything but something to hold plants up, but it is a dynamic living system that operates according to principles. If you have a nonproductive plot of land, and apply these principles for three years, you can have a paradise. The four principles are these:

1. Air and water management
2. Micro-life activity
3. Nutrient content
4. Mineral- nutrient balance

We try to find the keys that unlock the mystery of what lies beneath the ground's surface to enable the plant to increase its ability to absorb sun energy. Scientists estimate that there are over 1_ million species of soil micro life and we have only identified 9000 of them.

I could go on and on, but this is what I say to you. You have to find the correct principles on which to build your life, set your course, and you will be successful. If you will just take the Book of Proverbs and read from it every day for a month, start over the next month and do it twice more, after three months you can write your mission statement based on guiding principles. I am here to exemplify Christ. The tools I need were given at creation.

Write It Down

by Brian Hopewell

Brian's guidance counselor told him he would never go anywhere in life without a high school diploma. Leaving high school after 10th grade to enter Simon's Rock College was an unconventional move, but Brian couldn't wait to find kindred souls who loved learning. Perhaps he sent a postcard to that counselor from his year at the University of Edinburgh in Scotland or from his current position as director of admissions for the Sea Education Association (SEA) in Woods Hole, Massachusetts.

Sea Semester can take you on a rigorous ocean adventure in the Atlantic or soon, the Pacific. Brian takes advantage of his position to experience what students learn, and reports with delight that 20 dolphins surfaced and followed the ship when he took out his "torturously learned" bagpipes.

A man of many talents, he has several writing projects "in various stages of incompletion"— from folklore to a novel about a "peculiar relationship" between a Roman philosopher named Boethius and the barbarian Emperor Theodoric. Brian's children are home-schooled. They are undoubtedly enriched by their life with a wildly imaginative father.

As a younger fellow, I used to have a pretty bad stammer. Talking with close friends and family members was usually easy. Public speaking, however, was verbal Kryptonite for me, especially if I was in any way excited or nervous. Kryptonite, you'll recall, was the stuff that kept Superman from catching bullets with his bicuspids. If I had to speak in public, I'd jibber like a chimp.

The summer before I started college, I happened to meet my seventh grade English teacher outside the town library. She was a kind soul and a fierce defender of proper usage and grammar. I loved her for not seeming at all surprised to hear that I had been admitted to a fancy college. She asked if I was nervous. "P-p-petrified," I said.

I loved her even more for what she told me next because I think it may have saved me from a career in village idiocy. "Let me give you a little free advice," she said, patting my arm. "Before each of your classes, write a question down on a piece of paper. Write a complete sentence. You know how; I taught you. When your professor stops talking and asks if anyone has a question, put your hand in the air. This is the moment teachers dread because we're petrified that no one will raise their hand. If you raise yours first and recite your question, the professor will see that you're prepared, your classmates will see that you're brave, and you'll see that the day has not been wasted. Trust me, Brian, this works like a charm."

It worked like a charm. The first class was the hardest. The professor, a bearded fellow in khaki and tweed, almost didn't see my hand quivering a few inches from my right ear. But as luck or fate would have it, mine was the only hand that had reached even that timid altitude. The professor looked immediately relieved. It didn't seem to matter that my recited question was barely audible and wholly mundane. ("Wh-wh-what else would you r-r-recommend that we r-read, in addition to the t-text?") It was a complete sentence, the professor responded graciously, and I left the class with an answer to my question. If memory serves, I seem to recall an admiring glance from a girl sitting to my left at the seminar table.

I used this technique in every class I had that year. The formula never varied. Write it down. Keep it simple. Go first. I passed everything, too, except for French. There are some obstacles you can turn into opportunities, and some you just have to jibber through.

SM+G4=WP

by George Forrest

When George carried the Olympic Torch in Maryland in 1996, he had earned the right through a life of service to country, state, county and town. For 21 years he had an Army career during which he won many awards for gallantry, including the Silver Star. He served as Commander of the guard at the Tomb of the Unknown Soldier, and as a planner for the North Atlantic Treaty Organization.

George returned to St. Mary's County, Maryland, where he grew up, and has served as a coach and dean of students at St. Mary's Ryken High School. He works with local church and community programs to help at-risk students and teen parents. He consults nationally in areas of leadership development, conflict resolution, gang awareness, African-American male issues and insights on the Viet Nam war.

During the Viet Nam War, he found himself in the bloodiest battle U.S. troops had to fight—the battle of Ia Drang Valley—described in the book, We Were Soldiers Once...And Young. People who have borne great trials together keep a strong bond. The veterans of that battle continue to meet yearly in Washington, D.C. to honor those who did not return. A graduate of Morgan State University, he credits his own father for being a tremendous role model.

THE ABOVE equation means: self-maintenance plus four growth areas equals a whole person. The four critical areas that I have tried to impress upon the young people in my schools and programs are:

Intellectual growth —You have to grow smart. Where do I have to go educationally so that my quality of life is improved? It's true that you will be educated by being out there in the street. Some of the young men I've worked with say they need to be just smart enough to get to their 21st birthday, and an outcome of their lifestyle choice is that by age 55 they may be dead. Street smarts do not take the place of formal education.

I hammer on people about reading. Folks used to get killed because they wanted to read. You need to have in your pocket of stuff those skills necessary to take advantage of an opportunity when it presents itself. You can't say to Opportunity, "Wait while I go back and get what I need." If you can't communicate properly or don't have critical thinking skills, you will crash and burn.

Physical growth — God has given you this body, and you have control over what that is. You have to eat right, exercise right and do the health maintenance piece. Don't put anything in your body that has a negative effect.

Social growth — This is the absolute key to why and how we are going to survive as a society. You develop your social behavior based on genuine interaction with other people. This notion of a melting pot needs to be downplayed. We're a salad. We need to understand that every single group contributed to making this country great. Democracy is the dressing that binds us together. When I fought in a war, nobody asked me about my ethnic identity. They asked me, "What is your contribution?" Whatever your ethnicity, you have to use it in a positive way by making your contribution.

Spiritual growth — We confuse religion with spirituality. I'm talking about your your acknowledgement of a Deity. I'm not talking about formal religion. In all of the great religions, the majority of the commandments are about your relationship with others. While the big lesson I learned in Viet

Nam is that war is the worst invention man has conjured up, I also learned in combat that my survival is linked to the guy next to me. The same philosophy protects our society. If we don't understand our connectivity, all those people from the Revolutionary War to the Persian Gulf have died in vain—and that's a lot of people to waste. Studying and seeing your behavior in a spiritual way goes beyond the daily demands of your life, and you must actively seek it out.

Pluralism

*A free society is a living
laboratory of ideas.
Get an education*

Ode to *Four Essays on Liberty*

by Charles Krauthammer

Charles Krauthammer turns up on TV and in print when an independent and objective opinion is needed. If you were planning a career based upon his decisions, you would have to head for medical school, become a psychiatrist, a researcher, a speech writer for a vice president, and move on to become a full-time journalist. Charles attended McGill University in Montreal where he grew up, then moved on to study politics at Oxford and medicine at Harvard.

The turn in his career came when he moved to Washington, D.C. to direct planning in psychiatric research for the Carter administration. When opportunities to write came his way, psychiatry lost a researcher and the country gained a columnist who could look at political behavior from a unique perspective. He has won a Pulitzer Prize for distinguished commentary, and has been named one of the most influential journalists in this country. Krauthammer makes people think about both sides of an issue, bringing to bear the mind of a scientific researcher with the creative flair of a fine writer. His essay, which appeared in his syndicated column, sets the tone for the range of backgrounds and the variety of messages in this book.

NOT TOO MANY people can point to a specific day when they sat down with a book and got up cured of the stupidities of youth. I can. I was 19. The book was *Four Essays on Liberty*. The author was Isaiah Berlin.

Berlin was one of the great political philosophers of his time. Yet he never produced a single great tome. He left behind essays. But what essays. His most famous is "The Hedgehog and the Fox," a wonderfully imaginative division of the great thinkers of history into those who have one big idea (hedgehogs) and those who have many small ones (foxes).

Berlin was partial to foxes. He believed that single issues, fixed ideas, single-minded ideologies are dangerous, the royal road to arrogance and inhumanity. Against those who proclaimed they had found the one true path to political salvation, Berlin stood in the way, a champion of pluralism, the many-pathed way.

Four Essays on Liberty is his great argument for pluralism. Why was it such a powerful book? It came out in 1969. In 1969, to be young was heaven, and to be seized with intimations of heavenly omniscience. It was a time of grand theories and grand aspirations—liberation, revolution, historical inevitability—and we children were mightily seduced.

The temptations were many. There was, of course, Marxism; for the masochistic, there was Trotskyism; for the near psychotic, there was Maoism. And apart from Marxism and its variants, there was the lure of such philosophers as Rousseau, the great theorist of mass democracy and the supremacy of the "popular will."

In the midst of all this craziness, along comes Berlin and says: Look, this is all very nice, but what the monists—the believers in the one true truth, Marx and Rousseau and (by implication) such Third World deities as Mao and Ho and Castro—are proclaiming is not freedom. What they offer may be glorious and uplifting and just. But freedom is something very different. Freedom is being left alone. Freedom is a sphere of autonomy, an inviolable political space that no authority may invade.

In fact, said Berlin, these other "higher" pseudo-freedoms peddled by the monist prophets are very dangerous. They proclaim one true value above all else—equality in Marx, fraternity in Rousseau—and in the end the individual with his freedom is crushed underfoot. Heads roll. Millions of them.

And another thing, said Berlin: historical inevitability is bunk, a kind of religion for atheists.

And one more thing he said (in the fourth and final essay of the book): The true heart of the liberal political tradition is the belief that no one has the secret as to what is the ultimate end and goal of life. There are many ends, each deserving respect, and it is out of this very pluribus that we get freedom.

I read the book and a great fog—made of equal parts youthful enthusiasm, hubris and naivete—lifted. I was forever enlisted on the side of limited, constitutional government—flawed as it was and despised at the time as "the system."

Berlin's argument seems blindingly obvious now. But the anti-"system" ravings of, say, the Unabomber, which seem grotesque today, were common fare on the campuses of 1969. Today, history has buried Marxism's pretensions. In 1969, when history had not quite played itself out, Berlin's book was a tonic.

It was not without its flaws. It was brilliant in deconstructing the political romantics. But it did have its logical conundrum. Philosopher Leo Strauss in his essay, "Relativism," surgically exposed the central paradox of Berlin's position: that it made pluralism—the denial of one supreme, absolute value—the supreme, absolute value.

This paradox and Berlin's fecund, restless mind—which moved from one idea to another (often in the same sentence!)-prevented him from establishing a grand intellectual edifice of his own. He remained forever a fox.

But just as there are hedgehogs and foxes, there are creators and there are curers, Berlin was one of our great curers.

Basketbaru Has Its Surprises

by George Gmelch

When you park yourself in an anthropology class and a middle-aged, bushy-bearded professor begins to tell you about his time with Irish gypsies or the superstitions of the Trobriand Islanders, you might wonder if Indiana Jones is really George Gmelch.

Can you imagine trying to get through Stanford University while also playing professional baseball in the Detroit Tigers' farm system? Or living in a horse-drawn covered wagon for a year doing dissertation research on the Irish Travelers?

Ever an adventurer, George has taught in universities from Austria to Japan. As an active athlete, he learns much from the local cultures, finding a way to relate through sports. His students at Union College in New York are implored to travel and experience the learning which comes from finding themselves in new and unexpected situations.

George has written several books on baseball, the most recent being *The Ballplayers: Inside the Life of Professional Baseball*. Although baseball is the game has always loved most, he shares a lesson he learned about himself and Japanese culture in a basketball game.

SATURDAY MORNING in the Kansai-Gaidai University gym. Our sempai, or student leader, has scheduled a game against SWISH, a company team from Osaka. Finally, some real competition. After a month of playing among ourselves, this is the first game of the season. Being the tallest (6'2"), and the most experienced largely by virtue of age, undoubtedly I will be the starting center. Yoshi Fujimoto, adept, quick and our best ball handler will, of course, be the starting point guard. These should be certainties. But then, I've been surprised so many times since joining the club at the beginning of my sabbatical in Japan that who can be sure?

After the obligatory half-hour of warm-ups and drills, our sempai motions for us to gather in a circle. "Janken" (rock—scissors—paper), he announces in a loud clear voice. I can't believe my ears. My God, are we going to set our starting line-up by chance? Everyone pumps their fists twice, then throws out a fist, forked fingers, or a flat hand. As chance would have it, both Yoshi and I lose, while three of our weakest players are in the starting five. As I watch the older, more experienced SWISH players warm up, I know we stand little chance of beating them. They've been playing together for years, and sure enough, from the opening tip-off they control the play.

The SWISH manager began to substitute, putting his smaller players in the game. At the same time, our sempai sent in Yoshi, me and our other subs. The momentum turned, and we soon started to play SWISH evenly. But even in this real game, against a real opponent, the play never became physical; there was none of the aggressiveness that is characteristic of pick-up basketball in American gyms. At one point, when I lunged to steal a pass, I knocked over a SWISH player. The expressions of surprise—no one said anything directly, of course—made it amply clear that such forceful play was both unusual and unwelcome. Even when players were fouled, they never called it; rather, the offending player was expected to call the foul on himself.

After the break, the sempai assembled our team and SWISH in one large circle and called for janken. We were now going to mix up the two squads. I was beginning to hate janken. At home we divide players into two fairly evenly matched groups. Leaving the selection to chance meant lopsided teams. I fought to control my urge to try to make the teams more even and the game more competitive by suggesting we swap a player or two. My hints were ignored. Janken both avoids embarrassment by ensuring that no one feels less wanted by being selected last, and it reinforces the collective nature of the game by regularly mixing players up. Janken is also tradition; Japanese children are taught it by their parents at the earliest age, and later use it frequently in school.

Our mixed teams played three more games. There were no winners or losers because no one kept score. Not once did I hear my teammates express an opinion about which team had won or which player had scored the most points. It didn't matter. And because it didn't matter, the play-making involved everyone — with lots of passing. This, too, differs from most American games in which the best ballplayers do most of the shooting. The highly individual-istic, run-and-gun style of inner city American basketball would be incompre-hensible to my Japanese teammates. In Japan, the weaker players are passed the ball and expected to shoot just as often as the best players. " It is to make them feel included," explained a teammate.

After exchanging bows, followed by a few Western handshakes, one of the opposing players asked me how I liked playing ball in Japan. My answer, of course, was shaped by the cultural baggage I brought to the game. Reared on American playgrounds and competitiveness, Japanese basketball never seemed as satisfying. For me, fun is having good competition between two equally matched teams who are playing their hardest to beat one another. Yet, as I came to understand the underlying premise of the Japanese game, my appreciation grew. It is social and supportive, an athletic and group event in which everyone is not only included, but also made to feel valued. There is no place for stars. Players work together to perfect their skills and to enjoy companionship. No stars, everyone included — we could all use a little janken in this country.

You are entering a time of life when you are free to explore. To me there is no substitute for getting off the tourist bus and onto the playing field.

I Love These People

by David Isay

Log on to www.Sound Portraits.org and you are in for a treat. David is a master at ferreting out fascinating people and capturing oral history. He was once headed for medical school when he did a short program on a community radio station in New York. By chance, a National Public Radio producer, Gary Covino, heard that broadcast. He sought David out, encouraged him to continue on radio, and provided him with editorial guidance and a national audience.

David has made a career of learning about people, their problems and hopes. He has won numerous awards, including Peabody Awards for his radio series which followed the daily life of two young boys from the Chicago housing projects, and for a documentary on capital punishment in Texas. In June 2000, the telephone rang. David had been chosen for a MacArthur Foundation "genius grant"—an honor for which you cannot apply—based upon being selected by a group of people who have been watching you for years without your being aware of it. With no strings attached, half a million dollars comes to you because of the passion you show for your work. David was stunned by his selection, which enables him to continue to do the work closest to his heart.

He wants to share with you his love of unique characters on the edges of mainstream America. His essay is from the preface to his book, *Holding On*, for which he traveled to remote corners of the U.S. to find people who have something to teach us all.

IT WAS PROBABLY sometime toward the end of 1988 that I first walked into the offices of City Lore in New York. I'd just started doing freelance radio pieces for National Public Radio, and had already settled into something of a niche, producing audio profiles of offbeat characters around the city. I'd heard that City Lore was a clearinghouse of information about these sorts of folks, and indeed it was. At the end of the visit the organization's director told me about someone he thought I might like: a photographer named Harvey Wang. He went into a file and pulled out a list Harvey compiled, several pages long, containing the names and occupations of dozens of New Yorkers in no apparent order, more than a hundred of them: pool parlor owners, milkmen, ballroom dance instructors, gravediggers, pawnbrokers, elevator operators. I was ecstatic! I knew I'd found a soulmate.

For several months I pestered Harvey, and he did his best to hustle me off the phone. It took awhile, but he eventually warmed up. A wonderful book of his photographs, *Harvey Wang's New York*, was published in 1990, and I jumped at the chance to produce a piece about it for Weekend All Things Considered on public radio. It was the first time Harvey and I had met face-to-face, and we decided that day to collaborate on a book.

Harvey and I both found ourselves drawn toward particular types of subjects. Eccentrics, visionaries, dreamers, believers: men and women in pursuit of something, and holding on to that at all costs. These were stories of sacrifice, of quiet heroism, of obsession. There seemed to be certain qualities shared by all of the subjects but we couldn't pin them down. Was it the sense of loneliness? The bravery? Individuality? Resilience? Was is that oddly wistful feeling we were left with each time we visited one of these people? While driving a long stretch of west Texas highway one day we decided to quit worrying about definitions. We realized that was just a single, simple criterion we'd been using all along for inclusion in this book: these were all people we'd fallen in love with.

There were plenty of difficult moments on the road, to be sure: tire blowouts in the middle of the desert, a nearly broken ankle while serpent-hunting in the rattlesnake- infested hills of West Virginia, miserable, all-night drives, motel rooms where you have to screw in the bulbs for light, and countless truly lousy meals. But when all was said and done, at the end of the day Harvey and I would invariably look at one another, exhausted and giddy, knowing without question that we had the greatest jobs in the world.

Relationships

Whether with family, friends, or strangers,
every day you interact with others
and you strengthen or weaken
your bonds
with everything you say or do.

Derailment Isn't Permanent

by Jean Baker Miller

Pioneers blaze trails, but often must face the skeptics who disparage their efforts. Intellectual pioneers who take on established theories in academic or medical disciplines are able to follow their heads and hearts even when colleagues are openly doubtful about the direction in which they are heading.

Jean Baker Miller's work challenged the historically male-dominated field of psychotherapy, but she also found problems with the aspects of feminism wherein women were encouraged to emulate men. Her book, *Toward a New Psychology of Women*, was her groundbreaking effort. Ultimately, Jean's work enlightens both sexes in a culture which sends confusing and conflicting messages to the young about sexuality and relationships.

The Healing Connection, co-authored with Irene Stiver, continues to stress the importance of relationships in developing a healthy personality. Jean is a medical doctor and clinical professor of psychiatry at Boston University. The Jean Baker Miller Training Institute, part of the Stone Center at Wellesley College, is a testimony to her efforts to educate people in order to prevent psychological problems and build relationships that are affirming and supportive.

THERE WILL BE times in your life when you are going to be emotionally derailed. In many instances, a relationship will be at the root of your problem.

I was trained as a therapist through traditional psychological theory in which the primary goal in one's psychological development was to build a strong separate and independent identity. That left me feeling there was a large piece missing in the psychological puzzle. Until I began working with a group of clinicians that shared my frustration, I did not have the concepts or the evidence to form a new view which would help my patients.

The complexity of the world you face increases as people leave extended family, strong religious systems or unique cultures to launch themselves into a world where it seems that no one really understands or cares. Our new way of viewing derailments in human development involves the concepts of connection and disconnection. Crushing disappointments and devaluing oneself may occur as a result of a disconnection, and can often be traced to relationships that were full of roadblocks. We form our ideas of who and what we are, not in separating from others, but within the mutual interplay of relationships with others.

How do you know you are in a healthy, growth-fostering relationship? Young adults choose partners and mates, and make decisions that have deep emotional consequences. Evaluate your relationships in terms of whether there is mutual empathy that allows for freedom of emotional expression and helps you to accept yourself and the other person. Respond as accurately as you can to what the other person is feeling, and share your own thoughts honestly.

From mutual empathy flows mutual empowerment. The courage to live fully in a relationship comes from feeling empowered by it. We have defined at least five components to help you:

Zest: When people make emotional connections, they are energized, happy to be together, and full of mutual respect and vitality.

Action: You feel empowered to help each other meet goals.

Knowledge: You learn more about one another, enabling you to be a source of support as you face new challenges.

Sense of worth: A healthy relationship increases your own sense of value because you are indeed valuable to the other person. Attention and recognition are as important to adults as to children.

Desire for more connections: An important connection leads inward for your own growth, and outward as you seek more growth-fostering connections. Your friend, mate, colleague, and yes, even your boss are affected by your ability to understand and support them.

You may be one of those teens for whom life has been a breeze—gifted with brains, looks, abilities or all kinds—or you may not yet have seen your life as a comfortable, happy place to be. No matter what the pain you may have suffered in your upbringing, it is never too late to seek out positive relationships, and to learn your part in maintaining them. They are all around you.

Remembering Our Elders

by Sue Seal

Turn the pages of the *White Buffalo Gazette*, and you will see the news of Cherokee, Kiowa, Choctaw, Comanche and many other Native American peoples featured. Sue Seal founded that newspaper in Haysville, Kansas, in 1995. Started as a local paper, it now is sent all over the United States and abroad.

Sue's heritage is Kiowa-Comanche. She grew up in the country known as the Indian capital , near Anadarko, Oklahoma. She is proud to be descended from Chief White Bear, Chief Big Tree and Chief Big Bow. Knowing the feats and history of one's ancestors is an important part of growing up as a Native American. A talented dancer, she competed for ten years on the Pow-Wow circuit and, to carry on the traditions of her people, has worked tirelessly to bring the Pow-Wow back as an important cultural event. There is a national circuit of Pow-Wows that includes demonstrations and competitions in native dancing. Sue has chaired several of them, giving her time to her belief in the importance of tradition, the closeness of tribe and family, and the lessons of her elders.

Although her father has a European heritage of Dutch and English, he strongly encouraged Sue to learn her mother's heritage and carry it on. If you visit the Pow-Wow, hear the drums and the singing, and watch the graceful movements of the dancers, you will appreciate what she has done.

FOR NATIVE AMERICAN people, life is based around our elders. They are considered the "wisdom" of our families, and they have the last word. My grandfather, Homer Buffalo Tabbytite, was the last remaining member of the Kiowa

Black Leggings Society. The members of this society have served in the United States military. My grandfather was a scout from 1917-1919. Sometime before he died, he passed the "right to continue" (hold the ceremonials) on to some of the younger veterans among the Kiowa people. It was a proud moment when the Homer Buffalo Tabbytite family flag was flown at the White Buffalo Intertribal Pow-Wow in Wichita, Kansas.

My grandfather was a very spiritual man and a member of the Native American Church. He would hold peyote meetings in his teepee about twice a month. At night, I would go to sleep listening to the voices of the elders who joined him in singing peyote songs. They would sing all night. In the morning I would awake to the same beautiful voices singing their prayers to the Great Spirit. I learned all about our traditional ways from my grandfather; he was my first "hero." When he died, I thought I would die, too.

I learned to make all my traditional clothing from my mother. She was taught by her grandmother. My very first buckskin dress I made myself. I can do beadwork, make moccasins, leggings, shawls, feather bustles and just about everything we wear. I have taught my daughters, Shelleye and Stephanie how to do the same. When I am in charge of a pow-wow, my grandchildren are always dressed in their regalia to dance. That makes me proud.

Being part of a dying race, I feel that all of these customs of our native heritage must be taught and preserved. As an adult, I have worked very hard at sharing what I have been taught. I'm sure that's what my grandfather would have wanted.

Small Talk is the Biggest Talk We Do

by Susan RoAne

Susan teaches you to break the ice. Her ability to share, inspire and motivate started in her first career as a public school teacher in Chicago and San Francisco. She points out that no audience is too tough for her because she used to teach defiant 12 and 13 year olds. Now a professional speaker, she trains graduate students in high-powered MBA programs and company executives. Her favorite activity is being the keynote speaker who sets the tone for an entire convention, helping others relate quickly in the short time they have together. Because everyone is interested in being more effective in conversation, Susan is a frequent TV guest on the major networks

What Do I Say Next?, from which her essay originates, is a book that is helpful to everyone, especially young people leaving a familiar world and stepping into a complicated new one. Susan's advice can help you overcome shyness and understand the mindset of your audience, whether you have to make that trip to the microphone or explain to your parents why you are out of money.

A loyal graduate of the University of Illinois, with a master's from San Francisco State University, she has continued to learn from her relationships, hammering out new techniques. She is truly a psychologist of conversation.

CONVERSATION IS the basis of communication. It establishes rapport and connects us to our colleagues, superiors and friends. Our conversation skills are vital, and they will become even more so in the future. In the late 1980s, Dr. Nathan Keyfitz, professor emeritus of sociology at Harvard, concluded that in the year 2000, most people will be technically adept, but those who succeed will be the "people who can talk to people."

The confident conversationalists will set themselves apart even more than they do today. Knowing what to say first and what to say next moves us to the next step of our careers.

You may hear others say that they "can't stand" small talk. Small talk is the way to connect even in situations where "big talk"—murder, war, famine, pestilence and Papal Edict No. 123—may not always be appropriate. Not everyone wants to hear our views on the deadly ebola virus or the latest border skirmish at a museum fundraiser for students of the arts. The big issues are important, but we must know the right time or place for them. Small talk is the biggest talk we do. It builds, develops and nurtures relationships. Conversation is how we strengthen the safety net of people who make up our personal and professional networks, our cardfile of sources and resources.

Small talk is how we exchange information, preferences, ideas and opinions on issues. It's how we break the ice and get a sense of who people are, what they like and what they are like. And it doesn't always have to be about small subjects. I've often seen people getting to know one another by having casual conversations about art, sports, economics, government programs or health issues.

Small talk is what we do to build the big talk. It is the schmoozing that cements relationships and success.

And Then There's the Rest of Us

by Jacquelyn Mitchard

If you've ever sat in a school assembly and watched other people win the prizes or been content to stay away from the organized competitions which at times threaten to overwhelm the lives of children, you would appreciate Jacquelyn Mitchard's approach to raising her own children. Having six children has caused her to question her own view of success. Spectacularly successful herself as a writer and still be trying to meet personal expectations set by her parents years ago, she's happy to raise her children to please themselves and do the things that give them genuine satisfaction.

A long-time magazine and newspaper journalist, Jacquelyn hit the big time with the book chosen as the first Oprah Winfrey Book Club selection. Her number one New York Times best-selling novel, *The Deep End of the Ocean*, was also made into a movie starring Michelle Pfeiffer and Whoopi Goldberg. Her collection of newspaper columns, *The Rest of Us: Dispatches from the Mother Ship*, was published to critical acclaim in 1997. Her newspaper columns appear in 150 newspapers nationwide.

Jacquelyn demonstrates how to draw on one's own life and share it with others in a way that helps others cope with the daily problems we all face. This requires a willingness to take risks, a forgiveness of her own human foibles and a genuine desire to make a difference. Perhaps you have never thought about how your own mother reacted to your early run-ins with a competitive world. Her essay may give you insight.

MY KIDS AREN'T PRIZEWINNERS.

Don't take that quite the way it sounds.

What I mean is, they play, but they play right field. They're cast in the school play, but in the role of the tree. Although they do have talents, they'll tell you without irony their favorite subject is lunch.

I try to tell myself that my children simply haven't yet found things they want to excel at so badly they'll give their utmost. Some of them are too young, perhaps. Some of them just aren't so inclined.

One of my sons recently worked hard at his basketball skills to try out for an elite team. Then, when he made the cut, he declined. I wanted to flap around the room like a bat with frustration, but got myself under control enough to simply ask, why, instead of, "Why, for Pete's sake did you go to all that trouble only to turn down something anyone else would consider an honor...?"

He likes the game, he said, but also a whole bunch of other things. Doing one thing three times a week would cut too deeply into his time for those others.

"What other things?" I fumed, thinking it had better be reading up on classical Greek or particle physics.

But the things he mentioned were unremarkable: board games, biking with a new friend. In other words, being low key, an ordinary kid.

They do not get this from my side of the family.

I've done my best to communicate my own fairly wacko competitive edge to my children. I've encouraged them to try everything from music lessons to juggling, and played every card, including I-paid-for-this-you're-going-to-finish-the-season, to coax them into building on their abilities. I've offered payola for good report cards and sent off for specialty camp brochures at the slightest hint.

But my sons, and their big sister before them, remain relentlessly undriven. They don't loaf during a game, but are not even tempted to sob or throw equipment if they lose. They're as pleased with their smudgy handmade science poster as the kid at the next desk is with his motor-driven model of the double-helix.

I know why.

I've neglected one critical step of the quick, easy directions to building your own over-achiever. I haven't taught them what I learned at a young age: how much you're loved is based on how well you do.

Now, don't get the impression that I come from a long line of cold, disapproving post-docs. On the contrary. My parents didn't have the benefits of education. They saw absolutely no reason—including our exhaustion and our academic limitations—why their children should not do better. When we said we couldn't do it, they reminded us plainly that we could, or else.

I don't do that. I'm not draping the stole of parental sanctity around my shoulders. I just can't whip up the froth for it. I don't have the stomach to withdraw enough approval so that they'd do something just to measure up in my eyes-though they do care what I think of them. They know I'm going to love them just as much in tenth place as second.

Though some children are simply born to strive in their areas of excellence, behind most prodigies—from Mozart to Tiger Woods—there stands a hog-wild parent.

I'd like to say how happy and well-adjusted it makes me feel to think I'm not quite that. But that wouldn't be true. I've always thought of my kids' sorta-okay attitude toward achievement as the dark side of unconditional love. At school award assemblies, seated beside parents whose kids' resumes already boast more honors than mine ever will, I have to fight the urge to squirm like a carp.

To the bottom of my mind and the threshold of my soul, I know it is right to advise your offspring to do their best rather than to be the best.

But that's small consolation when yours win the "Most Improved" ribbon and your best friend's are the Most Valuable Player.

Still, even if they sense a wince, they go their own way. Some of that is rebellion, some is realism. We told them they had the right to define themselves separately from us. They don't forget it.

At times like these, I have to ask whose self-esteem am I worried about? Mine? Theirs?

Yes. Mine and theirs.

I do want to purr under the kind of approval a parent feels when a child does marvelous things. It says to you and to the world, "Well done! You're doing something right."

And I also worry, for their sakes, that they'll never experience such a passion for something so that they'll ignore all the obstacles. They may never experience the thrill of that. They may also never experience the hell of that.

Most people do not in their lives. Most people spend a reasonable time doing something tolerable to have the kind of life they want.

Perhaps my children will one day sing to their babies, not on Broadway. Perhaps they will one day detail their own cars instead of design cars for other people.

Maybe they will grow up to be like Elise O'Kelly, a wise woman I once worked with, who was neither stupid nor apathetic, but got greater joy from her garden, her granddaughter and her buddy Peg than she got from one single second at the plant where we worked.

My children may grow up not wishing to change the world or even to leave a mark on it, but instead to celebrate and experience it. They may be the most likely to be satisfied instead of the most likely to succeed.

We all want better for our children than we ever had.

And in my case, I may be getting exactly that.

The Depth of Real Friends

by Donna Kater

Few teenagers can recall riding across the plains of Western Kansas on a horse or carrying a shotgun for protection from rattlers, but those are two of Donna's memories from her early years. If you grow up in a rural area, you learn to spend time alone. The empty, open terrain almost guaranteed that an intelligent child would read thousands of books and begin to write as a way of connecting to a larger world. In addition, a bout with cancer at age 13 caused Donna to fear for her life and her future, so her appreciation of every moment may stem from her joy at having the opportunity to live.

Just as the Kansas horizon seems to go on forever, Donna operates with few limits on her work with clients. A creative college teacher who trains counselors, educators and therapists, her primary work has become individual therapy. Donna has a gift for moving quickly to the heart of whatever is troubling the clients who come to her Wichita office for help. But helping is not her primary goal—it is teaching others how to help themselves, and carry those lessons in coping into the next challenging situation.

When you work with the confusion and pain of others, you must care for yourself. Donna attends writer's workshops, meets regularly with supportive friends and walks three miles every morning around a peaceful lake. If she could, she would probably take off into the distance on a horse whenever she has a tough problem to solve.

I T WAS THE LONELINESS that hurt, the ragged hole in her heart where thoughts of her friend used to be. How had it happened? She didn't know for sure. One day they were laughing and talking in the way that was special between them, and then the next day they were apart. Someone else was laughing and talking with her friend.

Because she didn't know what else to do, she pulled invisible bandages around the hurt and hid the pain. Pretending that everything was as usual, she moved through her daily activities, even trying to make the relationship be as it had been with her friend. But inside it wasn't the same. The wound festered. What had she done wrong? She didn't know. Certain that somehow this was all her fault, that her friend had recognized some deep flaw in her, she hid herself even farther behind the exterior facade of every life.

Is there anyone who hasn't lost someone they cared about in just such a way? A new MTV video, "Real Friends," could be number one the first week it was released. Maybe it would tell us how to take risks with our hearts while still protecting them, how to open them so that the most tender secret fears that we carry are exposed. I think it would teach us how to share our hearts, not just our time. Maybe there are rules about how to decide whether this person is safe to share your heart with, and that person is not.

Rules for Real Friends

1. The choice of a friend is a responsibility to yourself. We often just simply step without thought onto the slippery slope of convenience and slide into what we call friendship. True friendship is choice, not just convenience.

2. Imagine the ideal friend for you. What would this friend be like? Can you trust this friend? Do you like the values your friend thinks are important? Do you respect your friend? What is it about your friend that earns your respect? Would you like your friend even if no one else did? Do you know your friend's faults and accept them?

3. People say that it is more blessed to give than to receive. We need to share the blessing of giving with our friends by being willing to accept and give equally. A rule to follow: give as much as you receive; accept as much as you give.

4. The greatest gift of all is the gift of self. But to share yourself, you must know yourself. The magic of friendship is that sharing your deepest knowledge of yourself creates greater depth and more self-understanding. In the process, both of you grow into even more interesting people.

5. Intimacy — the sharing of your deepest thoughts and feelings with one another — erases the pain of loneliness. Maybe loneliness is safer than friendship, but it's not nearly as rewarding.

Exploring the World

The five senses work hard
when you travel,
but your heart
sorts it out.

Sacred Journeys

by Martin Gray

Imagine Martin Gray applying for a job.

"Tell us about your education, Mr. Gray."

"Well, I was something of a bother to my parents in my teen years, so I moved from the American Embassy School in New Delhi, India, to New Mexico Military Academy, where I actually learned how to study and focus, and it did me a lot of good. A fantastic geography teacher there opened my eyes to the possibilities of the earth. I spent five weeks at the University of Arizona realizing that wasn't right for me. Five years later, I did a semester at George Washington University, and then transferred to Georgetown. When I left there, I decided that my formal education was probably over. Ten years as a member of a monastic organization, in and out of an ashram in Haridwar, India, going and coming, traveling and speaking all over the world, and teaching meditation made it logical for me to be in the travel business."

"Uh, thank you, Mr. Gray, but I'm afraid we don't quite understand this."

Log on to www.sacredsites.com and you can discern that Martin Gray is probably still a bit of a puzzle to his parents. The son of a diplomat and an artist, he combines international savvy with appreciation of the art of ancient peoples. Deciding to spend his life photographing sacred sites all over the earth and bringing his message to the public, Martin gives presentations with his photographs, but that's not all there is to learn about Martin. His study of kinesiology and body movement combines with his own natural athletic prowess; he was one of the top ocean distance swimmers in the world, at both five and ten miles, and is a world class juggler. Your parents would probably be upset if you decided to have a life like Martin's but his contribution to the appreciation of sacred places cannot be denied. If you can find Martin at home, he will be in Sedona, Arizona.

WHEN I WAS eight years old, I began to have visions and dreams of what I would do when I grew to be an adult. Being a young child, I had not yet learned sufficient vocabulary to speak clearly with other people about the things I had seen in my visions and dreams. But I could pray. And my childhood prayers were that I might one day serve as a paintbrush in the hand of God, that I might shower beauty and goodness upon the world. This has remained my prayer for many years.

My own total and unfettered participation in the process of pilgrimage has brought me many wonderful gifts. Pilgrimage may be defined as exterior mysticism, while mysticism is internal pilgrimage. Such has been the nature of my travels. Wandering extensively around the world, my journeys have been fundamentally an inner exploration of my heart, mind and soul. While I have been concerned with the scholarly study and photography of sacred places, my primary intention has always been to interact with the sacred sites as a pilgrim.

The photographs in my book and Website were created with something called sacred geometry. Sacred geometry is inherent in all natural forms, from the nucleus of the atom to the arrangement of flower petals to the spiraling of vast galaxies. In ancient times, people keenly observed nature, recognized its mathematical perfection and sought to mirror that perfection in their own works of art. Many times while meditating at sacred sites, I have received communications as distinct voices, or as visions of stunning clarity. I experienced a profound love for a oneness with the earth, and an understanding that my own work in life was to serve and protect the earth with all my heart.

I am well aware that receiving teachings from the earth may seem incredible; they certainly were to me at first. At times I was extremely skeptical of my own perceptions. I had to remind myself that I wasn't the only person who had ever spoken about a living earth, or who had sensed the charged energies at particular places. Additionally, I couldn't ignore the fact that many of the greatest religious figures of human history had considered certain places to be special. Moses experienced divine revelation on Mount Sinai, Mohammed on Mount Hara, Christ in a cave at Quarantana and Buddha beneath the Bodhi Tree.

My book of sacred photographs is my bringing energy from the sacred sites to the reader. My purpose in creating my work has been to share the teachings I received as a wandering pilgrim who is passionately in love with the earth. Perhaps these teachings will touch you. Perhaps they will inspire you to love and serve this wonderful earth more than you have before. That is my hope and prayer.

A Slow Seasoning

by John Norman Harkey

If you've done something foolish and find yourself in court, you could be grateful to find yourself in Judge Harkey's court. Along with a formidable respect for the law, he has a special tolerance for young people and their adventurous mistakes. He will put you right.

Judge Harkey had his own law practice in Batesville, Arkansas, for many years. He was a prosecuting attorney when Winthrop Rockefeller, then governor of Arkansas, appointed him as a very young state insurance commissioner. Always on the side of justice for the little guy, he liked nothing more than to play the folksy country lawyer while demolishing a case represented by a high-powered New York or Chicago law firm.

His tombstone is already in place on his land, put there when he was in his 30s, because he knew where his roots were and would stay. A quote from H. L. Mencken serves as his epitaph, along with one word: Lawyer. He loves his home, looking down on a broad expanse of the White River. He's been threatened, stalked and nearly killed by angry recipients of his justice. Now serving as a circuit/chancery judge, he is a colorful, wise dispenser of law and order.

ABSOLUTE CERTAINTY about the accuracy of my viewpoint on all subjects stayed with me throughout most of my teenage years. It was only after I enlisted in the United States Marine Corps during the Korean War that I was presented with different thoughts in such a forceful manner that I began to question my positions. Marine Corps drill instructors are capable of very convincing explanations.

I was provided with travel opportunities in Korea as a tank platoon commander. There were a good many times when I was scared. But the real benefit was that my service experience exposed me to people who had been to a lot more hog callings and cockfights than I knew existed while growing up in the hills of north Arkansas. These people I met had been more places, had done more things, had read more books and had seen more of life than the people I had known. It took me a while to get it through my head, but I finally realized that I needed to go to more places, do more things, read more books and see more of life.

I've done all that now, and after the passage of about 45 years, I've decided I've reached average. Is this conclusion necessary before one acquires wisdom? I don't know about that, but I surely do know you need to pause a few years before you decide you know everything. The thoughts of youth may be long, long thoughts, but many of them are downright silly. Pause, and take the effort to learn something from those who've been there before.

You Think I Should Go *Where?*

by Ann Morgan

The world knew Ann Morgan was coming, just from the signals that propelled her out of her small-town Illinois high school. Elected governor of Girls State, she then became president of Girls Nation. A bachelor's degree in communications from the University of Illinois, combined with an MA in international relations from the Fletcher School of Law and Diplomacy at Tufts, provided all the credentials she needed.

Ann's essay tells you how she made the decision to jump into the unknown. She taught in Nigeria as a volunteer, then joined the Peace Corps staff for a governmental career. She developed programs for volunteers in Micronesia, was a trainer in Nepal, and became the first woman country director in Thailand. For four years, Ann was the State Department's director of refugee training and managed training programs for over one million refugees accepted for resettlement in the United States.

Ann retired from the State Department and now operates a Bed and Breakfast in Lost River, West Virginia. Her travels make her a special expert in folk art from around the world, which you can buy in her shop. She raises miniature donkeys as a hobby.

WHEN I WAS 18, I knew everything, or so I thought. It wasn't until I reached 21 that I began to realize how ill prepared I was for the world outside of my small town in southern Illinois and the womb of college. Working in my first real job was the beginning of my epiphany. That experience sent me flying back to graduate school, expecting that more formal education would surely make me ready. Once there, I began to apply to other universities immediately. Much to my delight, I was accepted to two schools of excellent reputation. On the same day, I received an invitation to join the Peace Corps, something I had investigated just for fun.

Thrilled with my letters of acceptance to prestigious graduate programs, I raced to share my news with a professor whom I admired and respected very much. He also happened to be a rabbi, a title which — in my mind — added much weight to his opinions. His response to my news shocked me.

"Go home and call the Peace Corps. Tell them you're going."

"But I don't want to go to Africa," said I.

"Yes, you do," said he. "You just don't know it yet."

Luckily, I took his advice and accepted the Peace Corps invitation to teach for two years in Nigeria. Thus began a 30 year odyssey which took me on assignment to schools in Africa, islands in the Pacific, mountains in Nepal, villages in Thailand and refugee camps all over the world. It has been a wonderful journey full of extraordinary adventures and exceptional people.

I often wonder what my life might have been had I not listened to someone who challenged me to do something I had never seriously considered. He encouraged his students to pursue their dreams, to follow paths less traveled, to open their minds to new ways of looking at the world and to never fear the unknown. He was a very wise man to whom I owe a great debt.

I am also indebted to the Peace Corps, where I began my real education. Many who have made careers in international work began as Peace Corps volunteers. Almost all of them say that they learned more than they taught, and received more than they gave. Peace Corps ads say it's the toughest job you'll ever love. That is true.

Mind and Body

*Wholeness comes from
harmony.*

Life and Energy

by Dean Y. Deng

You won't find many eight-year-olds already being trained in the art of acupuncture, but Dr. Deng was identified early in his life as a potential master of Qigong (pronounced Chee-gong), the Chinese art of life energy. He actually began practicing the techniques of this system at age three. By age eight, he was studying Kung Fu and was beginning to learn about acupuncture. He attended medical school in China and came to the United States on a fellowship in 1988. He is a co-founder of Qigong International and the Asian American Acupuncture Association. In his current medical practice in Chicago, he balances Eastern and Western medicine in treating his patients. On his wall are pictures of himself with famous professional athletes, some of whom tower two feet over him and depend upon him to help those seven-foot frames stay in balance.

A frequent lecturer, he offers seminars in the art of Qigong. His book, *Qigong—a Legacy in Chinese Healing* explains his philosophy and starts you on the road to health with a series of exercises known as The Eight Treasures. You may have seen pictures of groups of Chinese in a park doing their graceful exercises. You don't have to go to China to learn them.

IT IS NO MYSTERY; most of us want to be happy. How to achieve this is the big question. Happiness, of course, means many different things to different people. It might mean getting something you want: improved health, a good job, vacation, a marriage partner, a new car, a house — the list is endless. But through the ages, the wisest among us have said that people and things external to yourself cannot give you happiness or guarantee peace of mind. You are the only one who can do that, and it starts within. This state of inner happiness is of foremost importance in Qigong philosophy and training. A mind that is thinking happy thoughts and feeling confident is a mind that can nurture and direct the Qi. Every thought and emotion has its reaction or response in the body. Chinese philosophy does not see mind, body and spirit as separate. Everything is related to and a part of everything else. A negative mindset impairs your total level of functioning—physically, mentally and spiritually. Negativity cuts you off from your spiritual source, your sustenance, the life force that pulses through your being.

Happiness comes from a mind or soul at peace with itself. This state of peace reflects inner harmony and balance. It is a feeling of wholeness. When the Qi is flowing smoothly and freely through the body, vitality is strong and you experience a natural feeling of optimism and joy. This is actually the state of harmony we are capable of experiencing day by day. But as the Chinese characters Qi and gong suggest, it takes daily practice to sustain this level of joyous, radiant and energized living.

Humankind's need to enjoy life has remained the same, even as centuries and cultures have come and gone. Continuous love and joy is related to several key ideas. First, the supply of Qi is inexhaustible. Second, we easily can learn how to tap into it, develop and direct it. Third, we are far greater than we have imagined. The source of the Tao is within the very heart of our being.

It's pretty simple, isn't it? The way to live a happy, healthy life is to cultivate your Qi and indulge yourself in positive, loving thoughts and actions.

Grandfather's Wisdom

by Zina Jacque

When you send in your college applications, you hope that a warm, understanding person is on the receiving end. For years, Zina was involved in college admissions. The calling to ordained ministry would not go away, and now Rev Zina, as she is widely called, is a pastor with the American Baptist Churches, Inc. She served as the Protestant chaplain at Bentley College, with a special interest in the difficulties confronting your age group, and preaches across the nation in churches of many denominations.

She enjoyed a career as a college administrator, and is now the director of the counseling center at historic Trinity Church on Copley Square in Boston. A graduate of Northwestern University, Columbia University, and Boston University, she believes that everyone has within themselves the ability, raw material, and possibility to be accomplished and joyful human beings.

I GREW UP IN a household overrun with family. One sister, two parents, aunts, uncles and grandparents galore were always — and in all ways — everywhere. One of the most amazing of the bunch was my grandfather. He always had a story to tell, a quip to offer. One of his ready sayings was, "There is but one unique you. Complete and eternal in impact, you see and therefore you go." I knew all of the words before I ever had any sense of what they meant. I could repeat them at the drop of a hat. Now some three decades after his death, I am only just beginning to gather the importance of their worth.

Through his quote (which we later discovered he made up) my granddad spoke wisdom into my heart. I am unique! What DNA regularly proves in this latter day, my granddad knew intrinsically. No one on earth has the same combination of history, feelings, experiences, ideas, mind and heart as I do. No one can be a better me than me. No one can do what I am destined to do. And that's not all, I am complete. Everything I need to be, everything I am called to be, is inside of me. It has been there since the day I was born. All I have to do is believe in it, uncover it and use it.

Now, the eternal part was harder to grasp. Yet, physicists tell us that when we come into contact with other entities, our molecules intermingle. Once we have touched, neither the entity nor we are ever the same. Through my touch, I blend with what will outlast me and become eternal.

When he spoke, "I see, therefore I go," my grandfather was encouraging me to open my eyes and see whatever there was for me to see. Whether good or bad, difficult or straightforward, I must be willing to see. Then, if I really believe in my uniqueness and my completeness, if I truly accept that I can move into a situation and affect it, I will go.

My grandfather was right. He knew that the power to change resides within men and women; the power to help lives and the power to make a situation better is awaiting release in unique, complete and eternal ways.

However, he also knew that as a kid I did not always hear him. So instead of teaching by orders, he just uttered these words, "There is but one unique you. Complete and eternal in impact, you see and therefore you go." Never would he explain them; never would he tell me what he meant. Instead, over the years and miles, he let me figure them out for myself. I wish he was here to confirm my interpretation, but even though he is not, I believe I have it at least partially correct.

So, what does it mean to you? Of what importance is it to you that you are unique? Of what importance is it for you to know that as you walk through life, you have everything within you that you need to be, all that you are called to be? Of what importance is it to you to know that just because you exist — just because you are — the world is changed? And how will you use this information? How will you see? How will you go? My grandfather wishes you well as you think about these questions. How do I know? Because every time he spoke his words of wisdom, he did so with a smile and with encouraging eyes for everyone in reach of his voice. As you read this, you are under the sound of his voice and he is encouraging you, too. "There is but one unique you. Complete and eternal in impact, you see and therefore you go."

Mozart Rules

by Don Campbell

Your job is to create a person who can understand all of the world's music. You might start with a five year old boy, growing up in Texas with a rich tradition of church music. Then move this musically talented boy to France, where at the age of 13 he could be the youngest student in a music conservatory with a famous teacher. A move to Germany to be a church organist also would give him the opportunity to become absorbed in the operatic world. He might return to North Texas University for college, a school well known for undergraduate music, and then receive a master's at a highly respected conservatory such as the University of Cincinnati.

But he has more to learn—Haiti is a rich place to explore the drumming and chanting brought from Africa. Then why not become a music teacher at St. Mary's International School in Tokyo? Experience the Japanese court music, Gagaku—the oldest form of written music in the world. In Bali he might observe the natural flow of the dance in daily life. All of these experiences may demonstrate to him that Western culture has diminished the central role of music in life's passages.

Don Campbell was all that, did all that, and much more. A student of the brain, the body, and the soul in relation to music, he has integrated the world's musical history and the results of scientific research into lessons for neurological development, emotional health, and physical wellness. If you learn that Don Campbell is speaking in your area, you owe it to yourself to hear him.

Mozart's music is far removed from what you may hear as the car next to you vibrates with blaring bass rhythms. In case you are more acquainted with the latter, I want to enlighten you about the importance of the former. Recent research at the University of California at Irvine has demonstrated a positive effect on learning after college students listened to Mozart. Many studies and much research in France, Great Britain and the US all together make up the term, The Mozart Effect.

People may know me for my book, *The Mozart Effect*, but the historic, scientific, and current interpretations of the impact of music the book recounts are only a part of the joyful and complex enterprise of my life in music. Truly this universal language represents basic human communication across all cultures. Music is one of the most important of common experiences for your age group to share; your parents can be transformed before your eyes when they hear music of their teen years, when for a few minutes they lapse into memories and suddenly are younger.

What you may not realize is how broadly the powers of the great gift of music extend. Scientists are discovering not-so-surprising benefits to health, both physical and psychological, through experiments with sound. Music helps plants grow, helps children learn, helps your body heal itself. At the same time, some combinations of sound and rhythm may be harmful to the normal functions of your body. The most obvious health threat in today's amplified world is to your hearing. Our delicate instrument of hearing evolved in a quiet world. Today's headphones may be extracting a future price you will not want to pay.

You have already begun to stash away your own musical library in your head. Take a mental walk through the shelves and assess your range of musical knowledge.

I'm asking you to stretch.

My musical suggestions for the inevitable ups and downs of life include Gregorian Chant for stress reduction, and the impressionists like Debussy or Ravel to spark your creativity. Watch the faces of a crowd dancing the polka— it's hard to frown and polka at the same time. If there's a job you're putting off, like cleaning your closet, a Sousa march will shorten the task. Before you study, try listening to the allegro moderato of Mozart's Violin Concerto No. 2. Turn your right ear toward the speaker to stimulate the language centers of your brain.

What do I most want you to understand about music? I'm asking you to reach out and explore it in as many forms as you can—play it, sing it alone and in groups, listen to it in a dark room with no distractions, belt out a boisterous melody on a walk in the woods. Try to understand a raga from India or Tuvan throat-singing. Music heals, soothes, increases your brain power, and opens your psyche to a glorious world.

Raise Your Glass . . . of Water

by Michele Longo O'Donnell

When Michele was seventeen, she entered a Catholic nursing school program. Post-graduate work at Case Western Reserve prepared her for work as a critical care nurse. In the course of her work, she made a radical shift in her observations of disease and its connection to spiritual health.

In 1976 she started the Holistic Health Care Clinic in San Antonio, which dealt primarily with degenerative diseases. At 18, it's hard to imagine degenerating, but the habits which will keep you healthy or degenerating are already in place. Michele describes a deep spirituality that led her along through dark times. She began to change her "expectation of disease" which pervades our culture to a positive view of the body as an extension of the spirit, what in Eastern medicine is known as Life Energy.

Nurses don't usually start their own clinics, but Michele broke with the medical model by no longer seeing a person as a "liver" or "kidney," but as a metabolic whole. Vicious criticism of her efforts by the medical establishment has given way as the effectiveness of her clinic has been felt by thousands of people. When the at-tacks were at their worst, Michele refused to fight, and kept her eyes on the path she felt was put before her.

Her book, *Of Monkeys and Dragons: Freedom from the Tyranny and Enslavement of Disease*, tells her story and explains how you can take an active part in staying healthy.

I HAVE A BAG full of tidbits of wisdom for all ages. I'll share two of those that address physical health and emotional maturity and stability — one very prac-tical, the other somewhat elusive.

At the Holistic Health Care Center, we have discovered in urine studies that there is a common denominator to all diseases — a high level of ammoniacal nitrates. These toxins are a product of the breakdown of unwanted, unwelcome toxic protein substances in the body. Regardless of where they come from or their appearance, they always cause confusion, disorder and ultimately disease. Some of the contributing factors might be: drinking regular tap water, eating junk foods, taking in pollutants from the soil and chemicals from meat which we all consume. While we cannot avoid the presence of toxins completely, we can strive to choose our food wisely, exercise our bodies and drink plenty of purified water. In fact, to keep toxins from accumulating, drinking plenty of purified water is the single most important habit one can develop.

My second tidbit is as elusive and subjective as the first one is simple to understand. If toxins are the common physical denominators for disease, negative thoughts, attitudes and emotions are the common metaphysical causes.

How can what we think affect the health of our bodies? Consider your body as a city set on a hill. Your mind is the wall that surrounds the city, and your spirit lives within your consciousness as the gatekeeper. We decide what thoughts we will allow to enter through the gates, what feelings or attitudes we want to entertain, and we don't have to entertain every thought that passes by! "You can't stop the birds from flying over your head, but you don't have to let them build a nest in your hair!" If we wouldn't allow a rapist, thief or murderer into our home without a fight, why should we allow equally destructive thoughts into our "city?"

Consider this oversimplified but true illustration of what happens in an incident of "road rage." Someone cuts into our lane, nearly causing us to drive off the road. Our first angry thought sends a message to release more adrenaline, which causes our blood vessels to constrict, reducing the supply of oxygen to our cells. This allows the cells to die prematurely and increases the incidence of disease. It also causes two specific hormones to alter the electrolyte balance, thereby blocking absorption of nutrients into the cells. This will in turn scramble the heart rhythm, tighten the muscles throughout the body and, if allowed to continue, can even reduce the activity of the white blood cells battling infections, allergies and other forms of disease. In the course of stressful days, it's no wonder that we end up with symptoms of ill health and disease.

The principle is that we reap what we sow. What we send out, even in thought, returns to us in spades! Without realizing it, we decide for the good or negative that comes into our lives, and we need to listen to the thoughts that come to us. While it may seem tedious at first, with diligence and practice we can develop thought habits and response patterns that make us like ourselves better, be happier and healthier, and feel more in control of our lives. In a word, what I have described is called wisdom. The beginning of wisdom is the realization that there is a law of cause and effect, sowing and reaping. Disease doesn't just happen; actions and thoughts have consequences.

Trials

Today or tomorrow
everything could change.
When the testing comes
how will you
emerge?

Control is an Illusion

by Mae Martin and Dan Conroy

Conversing with Mae and Dan is a developmental experience. They truly can finish one another's sentences, and thoughts fly like ping-pong balls. Both graduates of the University of Colorado at Boulder, each has developed a career path and unusual autonomy. Mae and Dan both worked on a comedy magazine, *Army Man Magazine*, started by George Meyer, now executive producer of "The Simpsons." Mae did an internship on "Late Night with David Letterman" and was a writer on the startup team for the "Rosie O'Donnell Show." Dan's career has been in therapeutic education, serving as admissions and outreach counselor, and owner of AIM House in Boulder, Colorado, a group home for college students.

This exciting couple shares something about what they never imagined would happen to them. From it, they continue to question and learn, and because of it, they founded the Mclaine Martin Conroy Foundation to help fund a critical care unit at Children's Hospital in Denver.

W<small>E WERE TRYING</small> to make the best of a rainy week in Hawaii, and decided to take a long hike through a lush forest. Suddenly, Dan slipped and was dangling 300 feet above the rocky Hawaiian coastline, clinging to a tree root. Mae proved the Rush of Adrenaline principle and pulled him up. For a few desperate minutes, things were out of control, but then, we smugly returned to our illusion that we were in control of our world.

We turned 18 back in the big '80s. We used to think that in spite of what our elders told us, there were some guarantees in life. We believed that there was a clear-cut right and wrong to almost all of life's issues, and that people who couldn't accept this were either weak or wishy-washy. This is not how we look at life today. The illusion of control is a trick of the mind.

Our next lesson was a tragic one. Mae was working on the startup of the *Rosie O'Donnell Show*, and I was on leave from my admissions director position at a successful boarding school. We were confident about creating all sorts of plans, but an unexpected pregnancy changed that. Surprised, but excited, we prepared for the arrival of our daughter Mclaine. She appeared normal. We were overjoyed and brought her to a loving home. A week after she was born, we went to her first pediatric appointment. She had lost weight and the doctor was very concerned. A series of tests provided the dreadful news that she had been born without a functioning brain. Not only would she not live for long, there was no explanation as to how she was living at all! We took her home, family flew in from all over the country, and Mclaine died the following Sunday. We can't tell you how many times we cursed God and screamed, "Why is this happening? We did everything right. We were healthy; this is supposed to happen to crack addicts and alcoholic mothers, not us." Doctors were dumbfounded, experts from all over the country were consulted, but no one could offer a definitive explanation. Science was failing us, faith was failing us and we were literally on our knees desperately trying to understand the unexplainable.

It is almost five years later, and guess what? We still have no answers. Today, we just have a bunch of questions. Eleven months to the day after Mclaine was born, our son Quinlan was born healthy and vibrant. His wonderful sister, Grace, arrived last year. If you were to see our family on a walk some Sunday, you might think, "What a cute young family." Judging from our appearance, you would never guess the hell we have been through. How often we judge people based on appearances. "Wow, they must have it made, they have money, a great house, blah blah blah." How often our first impressions are way off the mark!

So what are we saying to you? If we could leave you with one gift or idea as you enter the next chapter of your life, it is this: life is full of curveballs. Just when you think everything is under control, things change. There are so many events that are beyond our control. When we were 18, we thought most things could be controlled. That notion seems silly now. Don't waste your time trying to control people, places or things; that will almost always end in frustration. When we are with Quinlan and Grace now, we appreciate every second. Without Mclaine, we wouldn't feel the almost mystical depth of joy we have with them. Do your best to live in the now, right here. This moment is truly all we can count on.

A Sense of Humor Helps
See You Through

by Robert Bjoring

Robert Bjoring came into the world in 1920, on the day women were given the right to vote. He grew up in a small Minnesota town, and while at the University of North Dakota, enlisted as a flying cadet in the U.S. Army Air Corps. He entered the Air Corps three months before the start of World War II. His incredible ordeal as a prisoner of war did not dim his spirits, and he continued flying until he retired from the Air Force in 1966. After he retired, he attended the Wharton School at the University of Pennsylvania, and spent his next 15 years as a chief financial officer for California public school districts.

Bob is an example of a person who has undergone three "retirements," and exemplifies the adaptable career pattern which is likely to become more common in your lifetime. He continued investing in California real estate, and faces each day full of energy and a sense of discovery. He was widowed after a long marriage, and now enjoys traveling with his second wife, Eleanor Crowder, a retired professor of nursing whose primary love is history. Also widowed, Eleanor was married to a compatriot of Bob's who was part of the same flying squadron. It clearly pays to maintain friendships over the years.

WHEN WORLD WAR II broke out, I was a 21-year-old second lieutenant and pilot in the United States Army Air Corps. I was stationed in the Philippine Islands, having arrived on Thanksgiving Day 1941.

On December 7, 1941, Pearl Harbor in Hawaii was bombed by Japanese airplanes from several aircraft carriers. War was declared almost immediately. The Philippine Islands were attacked and bombed by the Japanese air forces the following day. Shortly thereafter, the Philippines were invaded by a huge Japanese army with abundant air support. American and Philippine military units fought bravely, but even together, they were no match for the well supplied, equipped, highly experienced and numerically superior enemy forces. On Christmas Day, 1941, my squadron evacuated from Manila to Bataan, a small peninsula across Manila Bay. Fighting was fierce for the next few months, but ammunition and other supplies — especially food and medicine — were rapidly depleted. On April 9, 1942, the starving, sick defenders of Bataan were forced to surrender to the Japanese. With three other men, I was able to escape while our troops were assembling to begin the march to prisoner of war camps almost 100 miles away. It was the infamous Bataan Death March.

Although the four of us were able to travel on foot almost 1,000 miles, we were ultimately recaptured and brought to Bilibid, a civilian prison in Manila. In late October, 1942, 50 of us, all American, were placed on an old freighter and sent to Japan. There we were taken to a large four-story brick warehouse in Kobe where 600 other prisoners — British, Australian and Dutch — were already incarcerated.

Treatment was horrible. We were beaten and starved. No medical attention was provided, not even the most basic medicine. The worst part was the starvation and extreme malnutrition. By early January 1943, the condition of the prisoners was pathetic. Starvation and disease—mostly beri-beri, diphtheria and pneumonia—began to take a terrible toll. Every day four to eight prisoners died and their bodies were taken away in wooden barrels. My very best friend Billy, another second lieutenant from my flying squadron, and I contemplated the future and it looked bleak. Several prisoners just gave up and within a day or two they would die. Billy and I decided we were not going to give up. But how could we fight the terrible fate that seemed so imminent? We decided that perhaps something to humor us might help. We formed a club. It had only two members, Billy and me, but the name could make us chuckle no matter how dismal the day seemed; we called it the "I Like It Here Club."

Between December 1942 and May 1943, more than 300 of the 650 total prison population died. Billy and I made it, and we are both convinced that the principal reason was the sense of humor we established and nourished during these trying days. Both of us came home safely after three and a half years of this treatment in prisoner of war camps.

If you can smile, or even laugh during adversity, the world seems better or at least not as bad. Establish and use a little humor; you'll find it a lot easier to struggle through and survive!

Standing on a Jewish Corner

by Gabriel Rivera

A mother once emerged from a parenting workshop with Gabriel Rivera and commented, "I'm not sure he's really from this earth." A soft-spoken, yet imposing presence, Gabriel believes in the importance of rites of passage for all people. Taking on the cause of disaffected and demoralized teenagers, giving them a new perspective on their lives and challenging them with tasks they never thought they could do gives Gabe his own sense of purpose.

Gabe has worked in many different settings with youth — from educating migrant workers' children to foster care and residential special purpose schools. Working with street gangs in southern California provided Gabe early experience in psychological disarmament and an almost fierce support for youths who are ready to move forward, no matter what they have done in the past. As the director of a teen age program in Sisters, Oregon, he reunites families with ritual, metaphor, and uniquely designed experiences. His deeply spiritual approach comes from his belief in the soul's path and his role in clearing the brambles in the way.

ONE DAY, PERHAPS yesterday, when I was a child and not yet a man, I stood at the crossroads waiting for a bus. It was running late that summer and I was running hot when from behind, an old man spoke to me and said, "Where are you off to in such a hurry? Have you missed your bus today? Don't worry, perhaps there will be another."

His face was weathered and carved by the storms of life. His beard looked as if it had wintered many snows. I turned to the old man and said, "I've got places to go and many things to see, and judging by our ages, fewer buses left to catch for you, and many more for me." He responded and said, "And you so young, so full of life, so much time and space to fill. You speak as if this were your last bus." We shared the hope and expectations of more to come and not enough time to fulfill, both seeking to live life to its fullest. We spoke for awhile. It seemed timeless, yet somehow inherently familiar. And needless to say, I missed a few buses during that time. He spoke to me of his world and many other worlds—inner and outer worlds—the world around me, past, present and future worlds. And finally, when I did have to board my bus, the old man said "Young man, if you truly know who promised you tomorrow, then would you please ask a little time for someone such as myself? Shalom."

The elder came to me when I needed to see him. In adolescence, nothing cuts to the heart of the matter like the recognition of life's essential elements of "passage and initiation." Like the Jewish elder, mysterious, yet familiar, the human psyche inherently knows that something is supposed to happen, something is supposed to shift. In your life you may find dangerous brushes with death or a severe separation or loss. In my belief, these are initiations which move you forward. Whether others judge the events as positive or negative, legal or illegal, right or wrong, does not matter. The condition of your soul and the permanent change trying to occur are what matters. Initiation events are often buried in the shadowy areas of the psyche, and when they are ignored they drain a person's capacity to change in life.

In my work, teenagers come to me from these passages—some dealing with abandonment or abuse. They need to be embraced in the "sense of home," and need to be contained and healed before true rites of passage can occur. Once they are secure in their sense of self, perhaps some of their abusive experiences can take on initiatory aspects. The poet William Stafford reveals his view of this secret sense:

A Story That Could Be True

If you were exchanged in the cradle and
your real mother died
without ever telling the story
then no one knows your name,
and somewhere in the world
your father is lost and needs you
but you are far away.

He can never find
how true you are, how ready.
When the great wind comes
and the robberies of the rain
you stand in the corner shivering.
The people who go by—
you wonder at their calm.

They miss the whisper that runs
any day in your mind.
"Who are you really, wanderer?"—

and the answer you have to give
no matter how dark and cold
the world around you is:
"Maybe I'm a king."

Each of us carries inside "a story that could be true," that will be more revealed as we stand in the rain and wind, robbed of our usual coverings. When all else is gone and there's nothing left to lose, then what is left and cannot be lost or thrown away is truly one's self. And what stays secret inside everyone is that somewhere he is a king, somehow she is a queen.

If Your Fuse is Short...

by Mark Lundholm

He looks like an athlete, fit and strong, but he was once a scrawny, hungry, desperate young man. His quick mind was clouded by drugs and booze. A letter mailed to him would have been addressed to a box under a bridge.

People don't attend a comedian's show planning to shed a tear, but audiences report that they laugh and cry at Mark's dark comedy. His first comedy act was with a group in a variety show in a halfway house. For a year they did shows in jails, rehabs, and shelters. The group broke up, but Mark was hooked on the way comedy put his message across, and he continued to develop his act while he supported himself by working nights in a grocery store.

From there, he took his comedy presentation and motivational speaking to the professional level. He has performed in clubs, theatres, schools and correctional facilities for the past 12 years. He has made audiences laugh in 5 foreign countries and 49 of the United States. He is currently working on a book of his own, a full-length feature film, and a television series for HBO.

Mark is an example of someone who, as down and out as one can be in this country, took his life experiences and turned them into a positive force. Check out www.marklundholm.com and find the colleges where he will be performing. If he comes to your college, don't miss him.

YOU CAN SENSE the change — their eyes widen and their faces freeze. I have just announced the unthinkable, and the teachers are wondering if they should pull me off the mike. "Alcohol is awesome, drugs are great—they make you feel really good."

In fact everybody knows that people start drinking and doing drugs because they make them feel good. I'm just telling kids the truth. 18? I'm glad I don't know now what I knew at 18. I knew I was bulletproof and immortal. I couldn't hurt myself with anything I did. What I didn't realize was that I was a follower. Followers always pay somehow. Most followers wouldn't think of themselves that way, but if you're worrying about what brand of shoes you're wearing, what car you drive, or where you live, you're a follower. You're living life backwards if you think just getting the right job or the right girl will make you happy. Who you are allows you the opportunity to get what you want.

When I sank into the world of addiction, life became nothing but a hunt. I begged, I stole, I looked for a place to curl up and sleep. I needed to eat. Some guy who thought he was helping me out by giving me a dollar was only keeping me out there longer. When you're young, you're always chasing something—it's a natural part of life. I was chasing survival, and there came a day when I got tired of looking for my next drink and my next meal; the minute I finished what I had just scrounged, begged or stolen, the hunt started. Just like you can't give a butcher knife to a baby, giving money to somebody like me was like giving me a tool I didn't know how to use. Finally I hit absolute bottom.

I had stolen a gun for "protection" but I knew that I was at some low point going to kill myself. The day came, I readied the gun, and realized that my only choices were to die or get better. Instead of pulling the trigger, I decided to go sit in the lobby of a treatment place I'd heard about, a psychiatric detox hospital. I didn't want to get sober but I was sick of looking for food and surviving on the street.

    I spent 28 miserable, hopeful days in rehab. I spent 6 more months in a pathetic, wonderful halfway house. I was there that I started to volunteer to perform in jails, hospitals, and shelters. I worked hard at learning how to play again. I became teachable by making myself available to be educated by people who had lived longer than I had, people who had survived some of the same self-inflicted wounds I had suffered. More favorable results were achieved by making better choices. Life, love, loss, and liberty are by-products of good decision-making skills.

    "Just Say No" doesn't work. But you need to know that when it comes to drugs and alcohol, different people have different lengths of fuses. Some people can hold out longer than others. If your fuse is short, the price you will pay is devastatingly long. When using stops being fun, it never gets fun again. I promise.

Self-Discipline

*Although you no longer endure detentions,
extra chores, or make-work for lapses in
responsibility, your taskmaster is now
yourself.
If you are fortunate, your new boss
expects improvement every day.*

A Cowboy Toughs It Out

by Matt Schneider

The American cowboy helped many of your elders grow up and know right from wrong, good guys from bad guys. Today if you join the summer stream of RVs heading to Yellowstone Park, you might glimpse a group of cowboys driving cattle to their summer pasture, a refreshing 8,000 feet above sea level. Little piles of snow remain in shadows, and the air is crystal clear. Take a closer look at those cowboys, expertly using their ropes and guiding their horses, accompanied by border collies doing their instinctive work. Some of them are teenagers, tanned and in superb condition. They don't have accents that would make you think of a Western cowboy—maybe New York City, Beverly Hills or Chicago are closer fits. Matt Schneider is teaching the boys, helping them to understand the behavior of the animals under their care — and by extension, their own behavior back on the streets.

On the main ranch, Matt is raising his family in a log house for which he and some of the boys stripped all the bark. The boys live with Matt's parents on a ranch which extends from the Montana border into Wyoming. Matt is not only a true cowboy who would rather be on his horse than anywhere else, but also is a student of psychology who can help young men strengthen themselves for their lives ahead.

LIFE AS A COWBOY is all about instincts and challenges. I'm doing the same work that's been done since people domesticated animals. I hate to walk. I'm on a horse 90 percent of the time. When you have a horse you become one with it. You have to control your emotions because everything you're thinking goes right from your brain, right through your body, right through your butt and the saddle, and right into the horse's brain. The horse senses your fright and can try to buck you off. If we're going along a cliff with a 500 foot drop and I get scared, the horse starts to stumble and slip. But you have to keep going; you can't turn around on a cliffside path.

I remember a spill when my horse jumped across a draw and I hit my head on a rock and was drug along by the saddle. When the horse stopped, I was knocked out for about ten minutes, but I somehow held the reins and finally could see and think. I wasn't going to quit and go home just because I broke my nose. I just had to finish the job. You just have to keep going because it builds endurance and makes you tough.

The teenage boys who come to us are mostly from the suburbs. Kids in the suburbs don't feel needed, partly because they haven't been made to work. The instinct of putting yourself in danger is real, but modern life doesn't give instincts a chance to come out. Because many of our instincts get suppressed and perverted in modern life, these boys drive cars too fast just to get a feeling for danger. Working with the boys is a lot like working with cattle. Here we always talk about "Moo-ology." If the cows don't want to go somewhere, you make them think you want them to go in the opposite direction. Range cattle have strong instincts, so do teenage boys. Boys have instincts to hunt and gather and build. We make sure the boys earn their PhDs, that is, Posthole Diggers.

It's easy to think straight when everything is comfortable, but as soon as you are under a challenge, it is harder. You have to learn to keep your emotions under control when in danger. My father was stepped on by a horse and lay dying five miles from any help in a remote canyon. He said his prayers and waited to die, and when he didn't, he finally put his glove into the head wound that extended four inches into his skull, somehow got on the horse, and made his way out. He spent several months in the hospital and is partially paralyzed, but he still works as hard as anyone. Our society has suffocated the development of our instincts. Work is an instinct, and you need to do healthy work to feel right. A couple of days without meaningful work and our boys are fussing and bickering.

This country makes you tough. You just don't back up. You always keep going.

White-outs and Sucker Holes

by Wally Funk

Wally Funk could be called a superwoman, based upon her energy and wide-ranging accomplishments. She developed an entrepreneurial, independent streak as a child in Taos, New Mexico, where, when she was 10, she "got tools for Christmas" and built a tree house. She set up summer businesses outside her father's 5 & 10 cent store, selling her homemade bows and arrows, vegetables from her garden, and even rabbits to tourists visiting that historic area.

Entering Stephens College at 16, she was the top-ranked aviation graduate. She continued at Oklahoma State University, where she became the "Flying Aggie Top Pilot." She qualified for the Mercury Astronaut program, earning higher scores than many of the men who actually went into space. When the decision was made to send men only, she continued with an aviation career. She has trained in Russia with the Cosmonauts, and soon Wally will finally achieve her space travel dream—going into space in 2003 through a private program.

Wally has been featured on "Dateline," the Discovery Channel, and numerous other media appearances and in magazine features worldwide. She could write an entire book of advice for young people, based upon her work with the National Transportation Safety Board. She has chosen two concepts she wants you to remember. You can learn more about Wally on her website: www.ninety-nines.org/funk.html.

I GREW UP WITH Taos Indians. They taught me about the Spirit of Taos Mountain, which still grabs me whenever I see that mountain. My Indian mentors were always in tune with the natural world and taught me to go with my senses. We all can develop that skill, and any time I go against my senses, I pay for it. However, in the aviation business, I have had to learn to combine the wisdom of my senses with the good sense of the rule book. Let me tell you how I learned this lesson.

At the age of 18, I was flying into New Mexico in a tiny Piper Cub plane. Suddenly I found myself in a snowstorm white-out situation. In a white-out, you can't see in front of or down from you. When you encounter a white-out, you immediately turn around and get out of it. But, I thought Las Vegas, New Mexico, was just ahead, and I went on into it and tried to follow a railroad track. God must have wanted to keep me alive because I made it. The manager of the airport greeted me sternly, sat me down and said, "You're that Funk girl from over in Taos, aren't you? I know your father and this won't go any further than here, but you will never do this again." And I've never flown in less than one mile visibility since.

In all of the 400-plus accidents I've investigated, there's always something new in the way of human error. Don't think about your next stoplight; think about the one that is two or three beyond. There is something called a Sucker Hole in aviation. If you are trying to find a nice flat place to land and you see a hole in the clouds when a front is moving in, you may forget to calculate that the cloud mass is moving with the wind, and what you saw before is already gone. Just as you duck into that hole, you may find a wall of granite instead of a peaceful valley. We call that a Sucker Hole, we teach about it, and still it remains a cause of accidents as people try something when they "know better than."

Develop your senses and learn to trust them, but remember that the rule book can save your life. Together they are a powerful combination.

Dare to Discipline

by Paul Sebesta

Do you know what the International Championship Ironman Triathlon involves? A 26.2 mile run, a 2.4 mile swim, and a bicycle race of 112 miles, and Paul has done it three time — once finishing fourth in his class. He has been a First Place Master in three other Triathlon events. Such an accomplishment would keep Paul's name in the record books, but read on.

He worked as a National Park Service Ranger during and after he finished his biological science degree from Doane College in Nebraska. After earning a Master of Science degree in Natural Science from the University of Nebraska, he became a research scientist for the National Aeronautics and Space Administration (NASA), was the Biosatellite Lab Director, Shuttle Experiment Manager and Ecosystem Science Manager. When you studied about the creatures — from microbes to monkeys — that were sent into space, Paul was on the ground, directing the experiments. One of his other functions at NASA was to serve on the Disaster Assessment and Rescue Team.

Paul is one of those people who uses every part of his brain. He has been the principal horn player in the Idaho State Symphony, but his true love is bluegrass and he has entertained as a fiddler in four bands. Music remains an important part of his life. Not destined to rest on his laurels, he recently became certified as a Search and Rescue Pilot in Montana, where he now lives.

I SAY, "Dare to Discipline." Dare to take your body, mind and soul, and discipline them to achieve a new excellence within yourself. Dare to set goals beyond your hopes and imagination. Dare to run the extra distance, lift the extra repetition, ride the added miles, swim the extra laps. Dare to keep it up until you reach a personal excellence. Dare to reach beyond your coach, therapist, trainers and peers. How dare anyone put a limit on you!

I would dare you to discipline your mind and completely absorb a liberal arts education in a college or university. I dare you to understand our western thought of pro and con, plus and minus, cause and effect, and formal logic and dialectic as we have inherited it from the Mesopotamians, Egyptians and Greeks. I dare you to understand eastern thinking of circular relational approaches. I dare you to compare these and then pick a lifestyle of thinking and working within the pragmatic world that combines both worlds of thought. I would dare you to discipline yourself in an understanding of ancient Greek literature and in Shakespeare, and see how those thoughts and actions are still with us every day.

I would dare you to discipline yourself in the religions of this world. I would dare you to read, ask, inquire and study all forms of spiritual expression that humans have devised. I dare you to withhold making decisions about any of these until you have exhausted your search.

In summary, I dare you to discipline yourself to an open-ended search for excellence within yourself. I have known athletes (ironmen), scientists and engineers (rocket scientists), musicians (Bach to Bluegrass) and Holy men and women (all faiths) who dared to discipline themselves and found the real joy and sense of accomplishment which comes only from within. I dare you to come to the point of realizing that discipline creates freedom — the freedom to live your own peace, joy and sense of accomplishment.

Spirituality

Busy lives hinder us
from searching for meaning
but that could be
the most important
thing you do.

The Secret Garden

by Matthew Kelty

Winding over narrow Kentucky roads may be second nature to the locals, but it involves a surprise at every turn for the visitor. When the destination is the Abbey of Gethsemani, the peace of the countryside is made otherworldly because there are large buildings, many visitors and clearly human activity here in an atmosphere of total silence. For this is the home of Trappist monks, and they are part of a contemplative order. For more than 150 years, monks at this abbey have risen at 3:15 a.m. to begin a day which, fortunately, allows them to "retire at will" after 7:30 p.m.

Father Matthew Kelty was born in South Boston in 1915. He was ordained a missionary priest in 1946 and sent to Papua New Guinea, where he remained until he was needed back in Chicago to edit a mission magazine. In 1960, he "followed an old dream" and entered a contemplative order. Included in this life of prayer, reflection and writing was a 10-year stretch as a hermit in Papua New Guinea. At 67, he returned to the Cistercian order in Kentucky and has remained at the Abbey as chaplain. The Abbey of Gethsemani partially supports itself through the sale of food products, including a decadent bourbon-laced fudge, which can be ordered from their website, www.monks.org.

A CHILDHOOD MEMORY that is still fresh to me in my 80s involves an Easter egg. In days past, they used to make Easter eggs (probably a confection of sugar) about the size of a grapefruit or large orange, but they were egg-shaped, perhaps more like an eggplant, but white. At one end of the egg was a circular opening, fringed with tiny flowers in icing. The round opening was a little glass window through which you looked at the scene within.

There, in the suffused light that came through the shell, was a lovely garden, laid out with flowers and paths and pretty arbors and trellises. To a child, it was a garden of delight, hidden and secret — very much the sort of thing a child, and the child in every adult, would delight in.

We need a window into interiorness; we need access to the hidden garden. We need to have our imagination kindled and our fantasy struck by some vision of God's world and the spirit within — the garden of the soul, the home of God dwelling within everyone.

The egg is associated with Easter because the egg holds new life within, hidden beauty about to emerge. As Christ rose from the tomb, new life rises from the shell.

Russian art, in the time of the Czars, created masterpieces in this art form of the Easter egg — elaborate works in gold and jewels with filigree and ornament. But it is in the interior that the secret lies, and the child in everyone needs a window into that chamber, a capacity for vision that will last a lifetime.

Soul-searching

by Shana Aborn

College students, especially English majors, often long to work in the media. Shana began her magazine career by working as an assistant on a film magazine. And since someone has to make sure that a magazine has its facts straight, she was promoted to fact-checker, a thankless, nerve-wracking job that all aspiring writers should do at least once in their lives. That magazine was sold, so she moved to New York and has worked for *Ladies' Home Journal* since 1987, where she now serves as a senior editor. At 18, her plans did not include writing a guidebook on spirituality, but it seems Someone Out There had other plans for her. Her book, *30 Days to a More Spiritual Life*, takes an unusually lively look at how to begin the exploration of your spiritual self.

Shana grew up in the Washington, D.C. area and attended the College of William and Mary. For fun, she acts and directs in a local theater company, serves as a volunteer cantor for the Metropolitan Synagogue in New York City and watches "Junkyard Wars" with her husband, John O'Hare. A trivia buff, she once appeared as a contestant on "Jeopardy" and won a computer, a desk and two Chia Pets.

IF YOU HAD TOLD me as a teen that I would one day write a book on living a spiritual life, I would have given you the kind of "oh, please" look I used to give my mom. Back then, growing up in a casually observant Jewish family, I hardly thought of myself as a child of God. Sure, I enjoyed the little rituals of my faith eating potato pancakes at Chanukah, dressing up as Queen Esther at Purim, but the rest of it I could do just as well without. At 13, better known as my Major Brat phase, I announced to my dismayed parents that I had no intention of going through the bat mitzvah coming-of-age ceremony, even though it meant missing out on a great party. Why should I go to all that trouble, I reasoned, for a religion and a God that meant so little to me?

Then I went away to college in a town with a relatively small Jewish population. At last, freedom, independence and the relief of not having to practice any type of spirituality at all. Oddly, though, all that freedom didn't make me as happy as I thought it would. In fact, I found myself seeking out the little neighborhood synagogue at the High Holidays, avoiding bread and pasta at Passover and teaching my roommates the blessing over the Chanukah candles.

Lukewarm as I had been about my religious upbringing, it had still given me a sense of connectedness both to my people and to a Power greater than myself. I realized for the first time how much I needed that faith and sense of spirit in my life. God hadn't been ignoring me. He was just patiently waiting for me to come around.

I'll admit that I didn't suddenly change my ways and become a spiritual guru overnight. After college, I immersed myself in work and other activities, moved to bustling New York and married a nice Catholic man. Still, the seed had been planted, and I continued to observe the holidays and identify with my faith. Then I discovered a synagogue that welcomed interfaith families, and being in that warm atmosphere made me yearn to become more involved with Judaism.

I started studying Hebrew and finally had that long-delayed bat mitzvah ceremony, which meant so much more to me because I had chosen to become a daughter of the commandment. (My beaming parents couldn't have been prouder.) I also began looking for new ways to connect with my spiritual side, through song and silence, mindfulness and prayer and anything that made me aware that I was both part of the family of humankind and a unique creation of the Creator. Am I perfect? Fully enlightened? Of course not. In some ways, I'm still a Major Brat. But the journey, as I'm learning, is the fun part.

And that journey is what, in my own fumbling way, I'm encouraging you to begin. Whether you believe it or not right now, we all have a basic need to feel a bond with that Something out there, be it God or Spirit or the Universe or whatever name you want to give it. Especially in these current shaky times, it's important to realize that we are more than the mass of muscles and veins and dandruff that make up our physical selves, and to find ways to remind ourselves of that.

If you already have a strong religious or spiritual faith, wonderful; you're doing better than I was at your age. Even so, it's good to seek out new ways to express that faith, because spirituality should be as natural a part of your daily life as breathing. If you're still searching for that path to your soul, then the best way to start is to simply be aware that it exists.

So how to begin? How about by...well, being quiet. No, no, wait. I'm not trying to play Annoyingly Lame Mom here. But think about it. From the moment your parents dangled that mobile that played Brahms' "Lullaby" over your crib, your life has been bombarded by noise and movement. Between the frantic scramble of the school day, activities in the afternoon, parties and just hanging out with friends, there's rarely an idle moment until you finally crash, exhausted, into bed. Accompanying those hectic hours is a nonstop soundtrack of noise and music: lectures, conversations, car horns, TV, CDs, computer games, concerts and cell phones. Listening to the sound of your own soul is tough when everything else in your life is trying to drown it out.

So try to take some time every day. I recommend 15 minutes for starters, to be with yourself in sweet silence. Close the door, turn off the computer and radio, get comfortable and just be. You don't have to worry about what to think or do; just breathe deeply, focus on the quiet and enjoy. If it seems boring at first, that's okay, but hang in there. Once you start making it a habit, you'll probably find this daily break-time refreshing. What's more, you'll start to get in touch with who you are, deep down inside and that's the first step to communing with God and discovering your own spirituality.

Contemplative walks are another good soul-searching exercise. Find a quiet place to stroll, focusing on all the sensory pleasures around you, from the smoky smell of an autumn wind to the sound of your footsteps to the sight of birds building a nest. One central tenet of leading a spiritual life is the ability to stay in the moment, and these simple walks are a way to break away from the multitasking grind and be aware of life itself and the miracles in it.

These suggestions are only scratching the surface, of course, and I hope that you'll take the time to discover more ways to grow as a spiritual person. But whatever you do, please don't put it off. Yes, of course you can go through high school and college without silences and rituals and finding your path to a soul-based life. You can live your entire existence without it. But you'd be surprised at what you miss that way.

Practice Makes Perfect

by George Lair

Dr. George Lair has been training counselors at Drake University in Des Moines, Iowa, for most of his professional life. He and his wife Diane, a speech teacher, decided to raise his sons the old-fashioned way, combining the operation of a sheep and cattle farm with his academic duties. The bucolic life was supposed to present a peaceful contrast to the pressures of a university. That was until *The Bridges of Madison County* appeared as a novel first and then a film. George's quiet spot was adjacent to one of the bridges. When you see the film, you see George's tall grass, and occasionally these days, waves of tourists. In order to make the best of an unexpected situation, George's son Kevin, an architect, helps to stock a small art gallery by the bridge. If you happen to visit the site, you'll see llamas and lambs, wild turkeys and Farmer George.

George's primary research interest has been death, a subject we usually avoid. He is the author of *Counseling the Terminally Ill*, and has taught in a Chinese university where he found that compassion, love, and empathy with the dying are universal characteristics. George has worked in hospices, and recently added a degree in religious leadership to his education.

WHAT DO I KNOW now that I wish I had known when I was 18? That we are all going to die. Oh, I suppose I knew it then, but it was so far away that I couldn't let thinking about it get in the way of living. There were too many other things to do; I had to become "somebody."

If you want to be a good runner, you go out and practice every day. To play the piano well, you practice every day. And if you are going to die well, you must practice that every day, too. It has been said that if you don't practice while you have the chance, when you die you will have to take a crash course.

I used to think that I would like to die by getting hit by a train that I never saw coming. Then I would never know I was going to die and never have to think about it. But after working with people who are terminally ill, I have changed my mind. Many, knowing they are going to die fairly soon, use the time to prepare — to think about what life means and what it means to not live. Yet, why wait until you are old or deathly ill? You wouldn't wait until the week before you were to run a marathon to begin practicing for it. The more you prepare, the easier it will be; practice takes the fear out of death.

What is practicing to die? The answer lies in thinking about what death is. Dying is no longer being you, at least the you that you know now. When you die, you will no longer be the you that can go to McDonald's for a Big Mac, the you that can go out and have a good time, get married, have kids. You will no longer be the you that has a goal to be a famous novelist, president of the company, or the richest person in town. No longer will you be the you that lives in this world. Dying means letting go of all that.

So practicing to die means learning to let go. So long as you live in this world you need to be you— to strive, love and care. But you also need to consciously remember that this is temporary, that it will all end. You need to be ready to let go. It's kind of like a great vacation—you enjoy it to the hilt while it's going on, but when it's over, you're ready to go home without trying to hold on to what was.

I worked with a woman who struggled with this problem. She was a nun, and all the time she worried if she was good enough, whether she was doing the right thing, whether the others thought she was a good sister. She fretted all the time that others were belittling her. We talked about the time she would die, and she gradually became aware that at this point it wouldn't matter; she would no longer be here to experience the belittling and the fear of not being good enough. And then she began to practice saying, "It doesn't matter now either." She worked on doing the best she could, and then letting go. She learned compassion—to feel for others rather than always feeling for herself. She learned forgiveness—letting go of her own need to be Number One. She learned empathy—understanding what other people needed rather than always being concerned about what she needed. She learned unconditional love—loving others without worrying about being loved in return. She learned to let go of herself, to be concerned with others because in the end, concern for herself didn't matter. She began to practice dying.

To die means to no longer be you. Practice for that time by living for others, by expressing your love for those close to you, by being honest with others. Don't leave important things unsaid. Let go of yourself and you will live more fully and with more comfort, and when the time comes — suddenly or slowly, tomorrow or in the distant future — you will be prepared to die peacefully.

Final Words

by David Douglas

Born in Washington, D.C. in 1949, David Douglas now lives in Santa Fe, New Mexico, with his wife, Deborah, and their two daughters. A graduate of Ohio's College of Wooster, he also holds a law degree from the University of Colorado.

He now writes on issues associated with religion and the environment. His book, Wilderness Sojourn, written from the Escalante Canyons of southern Utah, sketched the spiritual values of wilderness—silence, solitude, awe and gratitude—and the importance of desert and mountain as a setting for prayer. In recent years he and Deborah have written extensively for magazines about people and places associated with Christianity in Britain.

One of the strongest influences on his life was his grandfather, Henry A. Wallace, an expert on plant culture, founder of Pioneer Hi-Bred International, as well as Secretary of Agriculture and Vice-President under Franklin Roosevelt.

Since 1988 David has headed WATERLINES, a Santa Fe-based non-profit organization dedicated to providing clean drinking water to rural communities in developing countries.

AROUND A DINNER table one night, I asked a close friend of our family a question: if he could speak for only one hour to a group of 18-year-olds entering college, what would he say? What would be the single point he hoped to convey?

My friend, born in Scotland, was a retired Presbyterian minister who had spent much of his life in agricultural work in India. "I would say this," he replied, with only a moment's pause. "There is something more enduring than the material world we see around us; that we are in relationship with some-one greater than us, who loves us, and even if some of them perhaps didn't see that now, I prayed that they would come to know that with time."

He remembered that at 18 what catches our eye tends to be what we can touch, see and control; the secular world's offering of entertainment and pres-tige enchants us deeply. The late teen years often prove to be a season of life when least attention is paid to prayer as we set sail in voyages of self-discov-ery.

The poet T. S. Eliot in "Four Quartets" predicted that

We shall not cease from exploration
And the end of all our exploring
Will be to arrive where we started
And know the place for the first time.

St. Augustine wrote of the destination even more explicitly in his *Confes-sions*, "You have made us for yourself, O Lord, and our hearts are restless until they rest in thee."

My friend was right, I think. Given an hour, one could do worse than stand up and offer this: Amid many siren songs, do not lose sight of an eter-nal home. If you follow a trajectory away from the faith of childhood, hold on at least to prayer. And hope that each of us comes to know in life what John Wesley, the founder of Methodism, recalled on his deathbed with these his last words: "The best of all is, God is with us."

Afterword

FYODOR DOSTOYEVSKY was confined to a military prison in Russia for four years for taking part in a conspiracy. The horrendous conditions are fully described in his book, *The House of the Dead*. Yet what did he say about his prison mates?

"Even in penal servitude, among thieves and bandits, in the course of four years I finally succeeded in discovering human beings. Can you believe it: among them are deep, strong, magnificent characters, and how cheering it was to find the gold under the coarse surface . . . My time has not been wasted."

Whether you make your living at a computer screen or as a solitary survival farmer, the people you know will enrich your life. The people who have shared their thoughts want you to experience a small part of their own lives. Everyone you meet can have an impact, as everyone on earth currently knows something you don't. Keep track of your friends, your grade school teachers, your camp counselors. Remember the person who brings your mail or pizza. They all have stories.

Sociological research tells us that when we are looking for a job or need someone to assist us, the people we know less well than our inner-circle friends are in the best position to help. They are on the fringe of your circle, intersecting with a small segment of their own. Their circles go outward from yours, encompassing people and places you don't know. The place where you do connect is your path to a larger world.

It may strike you as unnecessary for an 18-year-old to have a business card. Get one anyway — for instant remembrance when you come upon someone you would like to include in your life. The value of connection, building relationships with people different from you, has been reinforced over and over by the contributions in this book.

As you reflect on the turns lives have taken in this book, you will note that many people ended up far from their early plans. Enlarge your circle, take some risks and honor everyone you meet.

Jeanette Spires

Bibliographic reference

Dostoyevsky, Fyodor. The House of the Dead. Translated by David McDuff, Penguin Books, 1985, p. 16.

Acknowledgements

Harvesting the thoughts of fifty-three people from many walks of life has been a rich exploration rather than a task. Finding those elders who could speak to the principles which hold true no matter what was completely dependent on a host of friends who were blessedly patient during three years of my preoccupation.

Starting with my husband, Jim, who has broadened and enriched my life beyond measure, and my severest in-house critics, Scott, Ann, and Laura, who write much better than I do, and know my foibles best, I couldn't have done it without you.

To all those who helped me think ideas through: fervent thanks to Betsy Lancefield, Jan Leahy, and Deb Wadas, who challenged me to get moving, Laurel Vlcek from the Vernon library, Kurt Reichardt, who edited my too breezy writing, Bill Seldon, Gretchen Krugler Mercurio, Ann Lurie, Jane McClure, Marnie Doherty, Marsha Ray, Carol DeLucca, Turbi Smilow, Bunny Porter-Shirley, Wendy Thompson, Jim and Lois Bomba, James Rosen, Maggie Andrews, Gil Dorland, Julian Olejniczak, Jane Crosby, Jane McLagan, Marsha Ray, Ann Patterson, Mary Anne Diehl, Diane Crozier, Dr. Memo, John Ripley, Ellen Ward Scarborough, KC Gray Siebert, Lauren Moi and Elissa Larkin, all of whom helped me with ideas or introductions. Special recognition to Rev. Richard Schliepsiek for the sermon that planted the seed, and for his encouragement to proceed. Susan Kimball, Leslie York, and Barbara Poole were with this project from its birth and provided much needed moral support. Thanks to Gary Covino, who is not only a journalist but a great son-in-law, to my Berry cousins, who share the love of words and ideas, especially Clif, who worked my proposal over, to Ronnie for breaking some ground for me, and Mike, whose paper ought to carry this story. The English teachers at tiny Manlius High School made us diagram sentences, a lost art. To my own siblings, Norman, Greg, Linda, and David, who add so much to my life, and my dear mother, Leona Anderson Berry, who taught me that you have to take the extra time to do things right, arrive early, and stay to help clean up.

What Do You Know?
Website Information

Our website, www.wdykbooks.com, is available for your use. If you would like to send a message to any of our contributors, we will forward it on. In addition, we will happily receive submissions for subsequent editions of this book. Submissions should be mailed to the address on the website, accompanied by a stamped, self-addressed envelope.